DUBIOUS
DOUBLETS

DUBIOUS DOUBLETS

A Delightful Compendium
of Unlikely Word Pairs
of Common Origin,
from Aardvark │Porcelain
to Zodiac │Whiskey

STEWART EDELSTEIN

WILEY
John Wiley & Sons, Inc.

Published by John Wiley & Sons, Inc., Hoboken, New Jersey
Published simultaneously in Canada

Design and production by Navta Associates, Inc.

For general information about our other products and services, please contact our Customer Care Department within the United States at (800) 762-2974, outside the United States at (317) 572-3993 or fax (317) 572-4002.

Wiley also publishes its books in a variety of electronic formats. Some content that appears in print may not be available in electronic books. For more information about Wiley products, visit our web site at www.wiley.com.

Library of Congress Cataloging-in-Publication Data:
Edelstein, Stewart, date.
    Dubious doublets : A delightful compendium of unlikely word pairs of common origin : from aardvark/porcelain to zodiac/whiskey / Stewart Edelstein.
        p. cm.
    Includes bibliographical references and index.
    ISBN 0-471-22764-1 (alk. paper)
    1. English language—Etymology. 2. Indo-European languages—Influence on English. 3. English language—Cognate words. 4. English language—Roots. I. Title.
    PE1574 .E33   2003
    422—dc21

                                                                2002155457

Printed in the United States of America

10 9 8 7 6 5 4 3 2 1

For Debby, my daughter and muse
(1974–1993)

Her spunky inquisitiveness, delightful sense of whimsy,
and insatiable love of language were the inspiration for
this book, and for so much more.

Such is the exuberance of signification which many words have obtained, that it was scarcely possible to collect all their senses; sometimes the meaning of derivatives must be sought in the mother term, and sometimes deficient explanations of the primitive may be supplied in the train of derivation. In any case of doubt or difficulty, it will always be proper to examine all the words of the same race . . . and all will be better understood, as they are considered in greater variety of structures and relations.

— from Samuel Johnson's introduction to *A Dictionary of the English Language* (1755)

Contents

Contents

A Word of Gratitude

For the ancient Romans, the Latin word *gratus* had a cluster of heartfelt meanings, including "pleasing, pleasant, welcome, deserving thanks, earning gratitude, beloved, favorable, and thankful." *Gratus* spawned such agreeable words as grace, grateful, gratify, gratis, gratitude, gratuity, agree, and congratulate.

It is in the spirit of all these related *gratus* meanings, and the words derived from *gratus*, that I convey my sincere gratitude to all who helped make *Dubious Doublets* possible. I thank my wife, Lynn, for her support over the years while I researched and wrote this book, for her uncanny ability at wordplay (displayed, for example, in the discussion of palindromes and semordnilaps), and for her willingness to live with an inveterately obsessed linguaphile.

I thank the folks at John Wiley & Sons, Inc., including Sabrina Eliasoph, who steadfastly supported this venture, and editor Chip Rossetti, who provided excellent editorial assistance every step of the way, and spared you from protracted etymological ramblings. Thanks also to Melody Lawrence and David Edelstein for their editorial advice, Shelly Perron for her meticulous copyediting, Jeffrey Hutson for his advice on Britspeak, Suşumu Sakurai for his advice on Japlish, Chiqui Guiribitey for her advice on Spanglish, Dr. Charles I. Heller for his advice on a variety of recondite subjects, Ronald G. Fontaine and Sandee Molden for their research assistance, Joy Roman for her secretarial assistance, and Steven Grimalli for his technical support.

The person to whom I owe the greatest debt of gratitude, however, is Professor Robert M. Longsworth, a professor of English literature at Oberlin College. It was Professor Longsworth who, in 1966, set me on my etymological path. I met him when I was a freshman at Oberlin, eager to take on the liberal arts curriculum. When I had the good fortune to enroll in his course on the history of the English language, I quickly realized that my desire to learn about etymology melded with his eagerness to teach that subject as seamlessly as two words fuse into a portmanteau word. The etymological seeds planted back then germinated over the years, blossoming to bear the fruit which is *Dubious Doublets.* You will find Professor Longsworth's name embedded in the discussion of "mentor" in maniac/automatic.

DUBIOUS DOUBLETS

Introduction

A Darwinian Approach

In 1918, Oliver Wendell Holmes Jr. was presented with a conundrum. As a U.S. Supreme Court justice, he had to construe the word "income" in the context of the Income Tax Act of 1913. In doing so, he observed: "A word is not a crystal, transparent and unchanged, it is the skin of a living thought and may vary greatly in color and content according to the circumstances and the time in which it is used." Lawyers and jurists have found this definition of "word" so useful, not just in construing the nearly indecipherable tax code, but also in defining words in other contexts, that this quotation appears in more than two hundred reported court decisions from all around the country.

The "living thought" embedded in a word does indeed vary greatly according to circumstances and the time in which it is used. To take Holmes's metaphor a step further, that embodiment of a living thought derives from a root word, in which a thought was initially expressed; and that root word, by a Darwinian process of evolution, spawned other words based on the same kernel of thought.

To discover that root word, etymologists study words from different languages having a common meaning, called cognates, and work backward by deduction. For example, we have a host of words beginning with tri- including trinity, triangle, trivet, trivia, triplets, trike, triceratops, triplex, triple-header, triathlon, and trichloro-ethlyne, all based on the concept of three-ness.

Two or more words derived from a common root, such as all these tri- words, are referred to as doublets. Our lexicon abounds with them. The common root for all these tri- words is, predictably, Latin and Greek tri-, meaning "three."

But tri- did not spring full blown like Athena out of the head of Zeus. So the question arises: What is the origin of tri-? Cognates of tri- include the word for "three" in other ancient languages, such as *thrir* (Old Icelandic), *thrija* (Gothic), *tri* (Old Irish), *trije* (Old Slavic), *tráyas, tri* (Sanskrit), and *tri-* (Hittite).

By comparing such cognates, etymologists, like geneticists studying DNA samples to find a common ancestor, search for the ultimate root of all these words. As etymologists would put it, they search for the etymon, a word or morpheme from which compounds or derivatives are formed. The word "etymon" appropriately derives from Greek *étymon*, meaning "true source of a word," from *étymos*, meaning "true."

In researching these "three" words (whose history in English extends from "three," first recorded in the ninth century with an archaic spelling [*prí*], to "threepeat," coined by Pat Riley in 1993 when he coached the Chicago Bulls to a third consecutive National Basketball Association championship), etymologists, by this process of deduction, have determined that the true source of "tri-" words and other words based on the concept of three-ness is an Indo-European root, *trei-.

A Word about Indo-European

Indo-European is a prehistoric parent language that was spoken in Europe from around 3000 to 2000 B.C., reconstructed based on the family of languages derived from it. That family includes most of the languages spoken in Europe and includes a vast area extending across Iran and Afghanistan to the northern half of the Indian subcontinent. The asterisk before Indo-European root words indicates that they are reconstructed rather than recorded. You will find an index of these root words and their definitions at the end of this book.

If we look around, we find more descendents of *trei-. Doublets tracing their lineage to *trei- include the less likely words testify, troika (the Russian carriage pulled by three horses), and sitar (the Indian stringed instrument with as few as three main playing strings), to name just a few. See trivia/triangle for more. Thus, we can determine, with some degree of confidence, that all these words derive from the same Indo-European root, in this instance, *trei-. And so it is with most of the words discussed in *Dubious Doublets*.

A caveat: Since Indo-European is a reconstructed language based on deduction, etymologists do not always agree on the roots of words, just as we can trace our ancestry back only so many generations, not all the way to Adam and Eve. Furthermore, we have no written records of Old English extending further back in time than the seventh century. Indeed, some words are of unknown or uncertain origin, such as jazz, conundrum, penguin, chagrin, quiz, lollygag, and gizmo. In this book, I have incorporated etymologies that, based on my research, reflect the prevailing thinking of etymologists.

Mining the Lexicon for *Dubious Doublets*

By this evolutionary process from an Indo-European word root to the various forms that the living thought embedded in that root take on, we derive about 80 percent of the more than 500,000 words in our robust lexicon. This fact gives fresh meaning to Winston Churchill's observation that "words are the only things which last forever."

The sources of our words, however, are not limited to Indo-European roots. For example, some words derive from foreign languages unrelated to Indo-European (alcohol/artichoke; hashish/assassin; jumbo/mumbo jumbo; sherbet/syrup; turban/tulip; and zero/decipher), people's names (franc/frankly; jacket/jack-o'-lantern; and sherry/jersey), and place names (damask/damson and hack/hackneyed).

Word pairs having no obvious common root are dubious. "Dubious doublet" is itself a dubious doublet. This book is about such unlikely word pairs, arranged alphabetically, with more extended etymological explorations of related words.

In mining doublets for those that are dubious, I have researched the sources listed in the Suggested Reading, as well as my collection of more than fifty dictionaries, keeping my eyes and ears open for new doublets. Very useful were *The Barnhart Dictionary of Etymology* and Robert Claiborne's *The Roots of English*, but you will find the mother lode in *The American Heritage Dictionary of the English Language* index of Indo-European roots, and, as a separate book, Calvert Watkins's *The American Heritage Dictionary of Indo-European Roots.*

I drew on a variety of eclectic sources in writing *Dubious Doublets*, other than etymological texts. You will find, for example, excerpts from poetry by Ovid, Homer, Andrew Marvell, John Donne, Tennyson, Shelley, Schiller, Milton, and a New York City cabbie; myths from Greek, Roman, and Teutonic cultures; the Bible; plays by Sheridan and Shakespeare; novels by Rabelais, Mark Twain, Lewis Carroll, and J. K. Rowling; writings of Aristotle, H. L. Mencken, Dr. Seuss, Oscar Wilde, and Stephen Hawking; and quips of S. J. Perelman.

Gathering Distant Cousins for a Family Portrait

For each doublet, once I assembled the extended family members all derived from a common root, I somewhat capriciously selected two distant cousins, placed them in the front of the family portrait, so to speak, inspected their features, and asked: What is notable about their common root, what do they have in common, and what is the link between the root and the various words it spawned?

For example, in researching Indo-European root *ker-, meaning "head" and "horn," with derivatives referring to horned animals, horn-shaped objects, and projecting parts, I chose carrot and hornet as two unlikely doublets, even though I had my choice of an assortment of *ker-derived doublets, including cornea, cornet, horn, corner, cerebellum, unicorn, reindeer, cranium, corn, carat, and triceratops. See carrot/hornet for more.

My approach is erudite, without being stuffy, well researched but lighthearted. In choosing doublets, I avoided obscure words. For example, in discussing *trei- words, I do not discuss triamcinolone (an antiinflammatory drug) or trimetrogon (a system for aerial photography). I do include, however, uncommon words that fit in the etymological discussion, such as supercilious, pusillanimous, saturnine, misericord, borborygmi, papilionaceous, altricial, oxyuriasis, narcokleptocracy, syzygy, and bathysiderodromophobe. I also include humor (beyond the whimsical illustrations) whenever the opportunity presents itself, which is quite frequently. The length of discussion of each doublet varies, depending on where my etymological exploration takes me.

For truly hard-core word buffs, I have included extended discussions of words about words. You will find them in the following doublets:

abbreviations	OK/kindergarten
acronyms	oxygen/vinegar
eponyms	damask/damson
euphemisms	brassiere/pretzel
Hobson-Jobson words	chaise lounge/longitude
onomatopoeias	poem/onomatopoeia
palindromes	palindrome/dromedary
pejoratives	flamingo/flamenco
pictograms	menu/minute
portmanteau words	portmanteau/mantle
trademark words	hill/excellent

Some of these discussions take you to exotic landscapes (such as semordnilapic toponyms), and creatures dwelling there (such as entymological etymologies). These extended explorations, however, are not limited to types of words. You will also find discussions about a potpourri of topics including, for example, the origin of language, the development of our calendar, the source of Arabic numbers, mnemonic devices, rebuses, allusive coats of arms, vanity plates, former theories explaining personality disorders and night-mares, the religious source of "do re me," how cats see in the dark, the origin of Halloween customs, the mystery of altruism, linguistic prejudice against lefties, the origin of the smiley face, how fireflies luminesce, the unified field theory, why puns are funny, the legal doctrine of "res ipsa loquitur," why we write the letter M as we do, and why we dot our i's. In addition, by the time you finish *Dubious Doublets,* you will be able to figure out the common denominator of the following words: onion, twinkle, travel, squad, foist, semester, October, noon, and dicker.

One last word before suggesting approaches to this book: The doublets you will find here will appear unduly dubious if you don't know about Grimm's law, so a brief synopsis is in order. Jacob Grimm (1785–1863), one of the brothers of fairy tale fame, was also a student of etymology. In examining words derived from Indo-European roots, he discovered consistencies in consonant sound shifts over time. Much simplified, Grimm's law provides a formula describing the regular consonant changes in words based on Indo-European roots, such as the shift from k to h, which explains how both "cornet" and "horn" derive from *ker-.

Other examples of Grimm's law are the evolution from p to f (pedal and foot), b to p (labial and lip), f to b (fundamental and bot-tom), h to g (host and guest), g to k (genuflect and knee), t to th (triple and three), d to t (duo and two), and th to d (thyroid and door). Thus, you will find in *Dubious Doublets* words having conso-nants different from their Indo-European roots, explainable by application of Grimm's law, but otherwise very dubious indeed.

Approaches to *Dubious Doublets*

You can take various approaches to *Dubious Doublets*. Turn the page and start with aardvark/porcelain to learn why the word for a low-slung, long-tongued, burrowing mammal is a doublet for a word for fine china, and explore alphabetically all the other doublets in this book, through zodiac/whiskey. Along the way, you will find cross-references to discussions of related doublets. Pick doublets that strike your fancy. Or turn to the index to explore doublets by Indo-European root.

Whatever approach you take, ask yourself before reading on: What do these two words have in common? This question can be puzzling, especially in such doublets as nostril/thrill and feather/ hippopotamus. In pondering each link, keep in mind the insights of Emerson, who observed that "every word was once a poem" and who defined language as "fossil poetry," and of Tennyson, who wrote: "Words, like nature, half reveal and half conceal the soul within." And consider Robert Kaplan's observation that "so many of our words are husks of metaphors."

You will find whimsical illustrations introducing some of these doublets, created by noted illustrator James Grashow. I knew I had found the ideal candidate for creating these illustrations when I discovered to my delight, upon meeting Mr. Grashow in his studio, that he had been exploring doublets graphically with the same zeal that I had been exploring them etymologically. (For instance, he had created a palm-of-the-hand-shaped palm tree before we ever met.) Examine these illustrations closely for clues to the common link. I expect that you will enhance your enjoyment of *Dubious Doublets* if you first seek to determine the common root in each instance, for the pleasure of the "ah-ha!" moment, before reading on.

aardvark | porcelain

The aardvark is, literally, an earth-pig—a pig with claws and an elongated snout, with a sticky extensile tongue over a foot long, like retractible flypaper, and an insatiable appetite for ants and termites. It is a native of southern Africa, where the language is Africaans, developed from the speech of seventeenth-century settlers from Holland, and still very much like Dutch. In Africaans, "earth" is *aard* and "pig" is *vark*.

Like the English word "earth," *aard* derives from Indo-European *er-, meaning "earth," and Germanic *ertho, as does the German word for earth, *Erde.* In modern Africaans, the aardvark is an *erdvark.* The only other words in the English language that begin "aa-" are "aardwolf," a striped, hyenalike African mammal that feeds chiefly on insects, "aah," and "aa" (pronounced ah-ah), lava having a rough surface, presumably from the verbal reaction to touching hot lava.

The second syllable of "aardvark" derives from Indo-European *porko-, meaning "young pig." In Middle Dutch, *varken* means "small pig." Our words pork, porcine, porcupine, and porpoise all derive from this same root, as does porcelain, although not obviously so.

In Latin, *porcus* meant "pig" (think of Porky Pig), *porca* meant "sow," and diminutive *porcella* meant "young sow." The transition from pigs to fine china evolved in France, when gastronomes observed the resemblance of the shape of the cowry shell to a pig's back. In French, *porcelaine* meant "the cowry," a tropical gastropod with a glossy, often brightly marked shell. Porcelain, the hard, shiny ceramic also known as china, has an appearance similar to the cowry shell, and thus we have the word "porcelain" for fine china.

Incidentally, "china" for dishware derives from Qin, the name of the dynasty that ruled China in the third century B.C. The English word derives from Persian *chini*. When "china" first appeared in English, it was variously spelled "chiney," "cheny," and "cheney."

Next time you dine on fine china, you may think of Porky Pig, cowry shells or, to more disastrous effect, the aardvark's monstrous tongue foraging underground for ants.

admonish | money

Juno was the Roman version of the earth mother, the supreme goddess in the Roman hierarchy. One of Juno's surnames was "Moneta"—she who warns—from Latin *monere*, to warn. According to ancient Roman legend, Juno's sacred geese gave the alarm when invading Gauls tried to take Rome in 390 B.C. About a hundred years later, the Romans appealed to Juno for advice in a battle with King Pyrrhus of Epirus in 275 B.C. that resulted, eponymously, in his Pyrrhic victory (a victory gained at too great a cost).

In appreciation of what was effectively a Roman victory, the Romans held a festival during a month named for Juno, Junius mensis (our June), and erected a temple to her, naming it "Moneta" in her honor. In this temple, beginning 269 B.C., the Romans minted silver coins. Referencing their origin, these coins were commonly called *moneta,* to distinguish them from copper coins. From *moneta* we have, as a result of corruptions in sound and spelling in Old French, our words "money" and "mint." From uncorrupted *moneta* and Latin *monetarius* (pertaining to money) we derive "monetary."

The "warning" or "reminding" sense of *monere* is found in such words as admonish, monitor (one who reminds or admonishes), monument (originally, a gravestone reminding passers-by of the deceased), summons (a warning to appear in court), premonition (a warning in advance), monster (originally, an extraordinary omen serving as a divine premonition), demonstrate, remonstrate, and muster (originally, to display).

All these mon- words derive from Indo-European *men-, meaning "to think," with derivatives referring to various qualities and states of mind. For other *men-based words, see amnesty/ mnemonic and maniac/automatic. For more on month names, see August/inaugurate and dean/December.

adultery | altruism

The etymology of "adultery" is linked to that of "adulterate." Both derive from Latin *adulterare,* meaning "debauch, corrupt," probably based on Latin *alter,* meaning "other." The first syllable, *ad-,* is Latin for "toward"—and so the base idea of *adulterare* is "toward another," more specifically, pollution from an extraneous source.

From this same Latin *alter* root we have alter (to give something other qualities), alter ego, alternate, alternative, alternating current, and altruism. Altruism, a selfless concern and willingness to sacrifice for others, evolved from this Latin root via the French legal phrase *le bien d'autrui* (the welfare of others) and Italian *altrui* (that which belongs to other people). In our society, sharing with another in a variety of ways is good (altruism), so long as it is not sexual (adultery).

According to most biologists, altruistic behavior is rooted in the human capacity for language and memory. The theory is that with language, people can learn of individuals they have never met, feel compassion for their suffering, and emulate the altruistic acts of others.

Some other species engage in acts of altruism, as in ant and bee colonies, in which sterile female workers labor ceaselessly for their queen, and will even die for her if the nest is threatened. Altruism gives profound meaning to the link to the "other" derived from Latin *alter.*

Only an adult can commit adultery, but "adult" and "adultery" are unrelated etymologically. "Adult" derives from *adultus,* the past participle of Latin *adolere* (to cause to grow). In Latin, one in the process of growing is *adolescens,* our "adolescent," in the same form as convalescent, obsolescent, and senescent.

album | auburn

The root of our word "album" is Latin *albus,* meaning "white." In Latin, an *album* meant a blank (white) tablet on which public notices were inscribed. In Germany, as early as the sixteenth century, scholars kept an *album amicorum* (literally "book of friends"), in which they collected colleagues' signatures and writings. Gradually, "album" took on the sense of a repository for all sorts of souvenirs, including photograph albums, wedding albums (which are usually white), and, before the advent of tapes and CDs, record albums. Etymologically speaking, the Beatles' *White Album* is a redundancy.

Related "white" words are the white of an egg (albumen), a person lacking color genes (albino), and an old word for Britain, referencing the white cliffs of Dover (Albion). The less obvious "daub" also derives from *albus,* via Latin *dealbare,* literally, "to whiten." This word evolved in English more specifically to mean "cover with a white substance, such as whitewash, plaster, or mortar." Reference to this messy process led to our sense of "apply crudely." The lovely but obscure word "aubade" means "a song or music evoking daybreak," or "a poem or song about lovers separating at dawn." It derives from Latin *albus*, via Old French *albade*, with reference to the dawning sky.

Auburn, also derived from *albus*, means "reddish brown" or "golden-brown." How does white become a brown hue? Auburn appeared in medieval Latin as *alburnus*, meaning "off-white." Via Old French *alborne* and *auborne*, this word passed into English as "abrun," "abrune," and "abroun." This spelling probably gave rise to the idea that "auburn" was a kind of brown. The sense shift was already apparent in the Old French variant *aubornaz*, meaning "dark blond."

The names of colors often shifted in Indo-European languages, so that names for different colors have related forms from the same root word. *Bhel-, for example, the Indo-European root meaning "to shine, flash, or burn," is the source of "blue," and evolved in Old Icelandic as *bla*, meaning "livid"; in Latin as *flavus*, meaning "yellow"; and in Greek as *phalos*, meaning "white."

Modern English words derived from *bhel- cover the color spectrum. The underlying notion is that when something shines, flashes, or burns, it displays a brightness and, especially in burning, a variety of colors. Our ancient ancestors needed a word for what they saw, and naturally that word took on a variety of color senses. Words derived from *bhel- include blue, blind, black, blaze, bleach, beluga (a white sturgeon), bleak, blend, blond, blanch, blank, blanket (originally, white wool used for clothing), blush, bald (think of the shiny pate), and blemish (originally, to make pale).

In our own lexicon, "blue" takes on many shades of meaning: blue-chip stock is generally a good investment, but we are wary of blue-sky stock; a blue-collar worker is a manual laborer, but a blue-stocking has strong scholarly and literary interests; a bluenose is a prude, but blue blood is aristocratic; when we're down we feel blue; we listen to the blues and to bluegrass music; and some people talk a blue streak.

The experience of "blue" doesn't end there: when in need of erotica, some choose to watch blue movies; when exasperated, we are blue in the face; we travel on back-road blue highways, and fly into the wild blue yonder; we abide by blue laws (such as those limiting Sunday activities); some events occur only once in a blue moon; editors blue pencil a manuscript; we eat the blue-plate special; winners at county fairs get blue ribbons; and when something unexpected happens, it is out of the blue. Computer geeks say a computer system is "blue screened" or displays the BSOD ("Blue Screen of Death") when the Windows operating system crashes, displaying an error message on a blue screen. And in Brazil, feeling "blue" means that everything is great—*tudo azul!*

alcohol | artichoke

In Arabic, *al* means "the." The two most important Muslim holidays are Eid al-Fitr (end of the Ramadan fasting) and Eid al-Adha (end of the pilgrimage to Mecca). Because of the achievements of the Arabic-speaking world at the time, a number of words borrowed by Europeans in the late Middle Ages and Renaissance were mathematical or scientific. Thus, a variety of words in our vocabulary combine "al" with an Arabic noun to create common (and some less common) words, giving insight into ancient Arabic culture.

"Alcohol" is from Arabic *al-kuhul,* meaning "the powdered antimony used as a cosmetic to darken eyelids." This substance was obtained by sublimation, a chemical refinement process. "Alcohol" came to mean "any substance obtained by sublimation." Thus, "alcohol of wine" was "the quintessence of wine" produced by distillation. By the middle of the eighteenth century, "alcohol" was used on its own to refer to the intoxicating ingredient in strong liquor.

"Algebra," from Arabic *al-jebr,* first entered English in the sixteenth century to mean the setting of broken bones, but by the end of that century its central meaning was mathematical.

A less common word, "algorithm," derives from the name of ninth-century Arab mathematician Abu Ja'far Mohammed ibn-Musa al-Khwarizmi, who lived and taught in Baghdad. The last part of his name means that he was from the ("al-") town of Khwarizm

("Khwarizmi"), now called Khiva. Al-Khwarizmi was the chief proponent of the Arabic system of numeration and calculation based on the number ten. The eponymous name for this numbering system in Arabic was *al-khwarizmi*, borrowed into medieval Latin as *algorismus.*

Under the influence of Greek *arithmos*, meaning "number," this word evolved into "algorithm." An algorithm is a term for any step-by-step mathematical procedure, as used in computers, quantitative-based models, and logic trees. Thanks to Al-Khwarizmi, we use Arabic numbers, and don't need to learn how to multiply and divide Roman numerals. An early computer language preserved the "al-" in Al-Khwarizmi's name: ALGOL, short for "algorithmic language."

Other words in this al- family include "alcove," from Arabic *al-qobbah*, meaning "arch, vault, vaulted room"; "alkali," from Arabic *al-qaliy*, literally "the ashes," from Arabic *qalay*, meaning "to fry" (alkali was originally extracted from the ashes of a certain plant, salt-wort, whose technical name is *Salsoli kali*); and "alchemy," from Arabic *al-kimia*, the art of transmuting base metals into gold. "Alchemy" itself lost its first syllable and its sense of such magical transmutation to become our word "chemistry."

"Albatross" may be from Arabic *al-qadus*, "the bucket," on the premise that the bucket of a waterwheel used for irrigation resembles a pelican's beak. "Alfalfa" derives from Arabic *al-fasfasa*, meaning "the best kind of fodder." "Almanac" may be from Spanish-Arabic *al-manakh*, meaning "calendar."

The Arabic al appears at the end of "admiral," derived from "amir-al," literally "commander of the . . ." Thus, Arabic titles included, for example, *amir-al-bahr* (commander of the sea), and *amir-al-muminin* (commander of the faithful). When borrowed into European languages, *amir-al* was misconstrued as an independent word. Over time, *amir-al* evolved to "admiral," the commander of the fleet.

The Arabic *al* root disappears altogether in several words derived from it. "Artichoke" evolved from Arabic *al-harsuf*, to Old Spanish *alcarchofa*, to Italian *articiocco*, and then to various forms in English, including archecokk, archichoke, archychock, artochock, hortichock, artichault, artichowe, artechock, archoke, artychough, artichoak, artechoke, and, finally, artichoke. The evolution is via Spanish because Arabs ruled much of Spain for several centuries during the Middle Ages.

"Azure" derives from Arabic *al-lazaward,* via medieval Latin *azura* and Old French *azur. Al-lazaward* referred to the semiprecious gem lapis lazuli, that is opaque to translucent blue, violet-blue, or greenish blue. The "lazuli" in "lapis lazuli" likewise gets its name from *al-lazaward; lapis* is Latin for "stone."

"Hazard" derives from Arabic *az-zahr* (the die), *az-* being a form of *al-* by assimilation to the *z* of the following word. "Az-zahr" evolved via Old French *hasard* to English as hasard around 1300, with reference to a game of chance played with dice, taking on the meaning of a chance of loss or harm in recorded form in the sixteenth century.

For other words based on Arabic culture, see turban/tulip and zero/decipher.

alibi | alien

When O. J. Simpson took the position that he was at home with Kato Kaelin at the time of the murders he was charged with, that was his alibi—he was somewhere else. And that is precisely what "alibi" means. It is pure Latin, a meld of the Latin words *alius* (other) and *ubi* (where). An example of its usage in the early eighteenth century is: "The prisoner endeavoured to prove himself Alibi." By the end of the eighteenth century, "alibi" became a noun meaning "plea of being elsewhere at the time of a crime." The more general sense of "an excuse" developed in the twentieth century. Now a person can have an alibi without being accused of a crime.

The same Latin root *alius* developed into the noun for someone from another country or planet, "alien," via the Latin adjective *alienus,* belonging to another person or place. The word "alienate," meaning "to estrange" or "transfer to another's ownership," developed in the sixteenth century. Other related words are alienable, inalienable, and else.

"Alimony" is not in this word group, even though it begins "ali-" and is money paid to another. Instead, "alimony" derives from Latin *alo*, meaning "nourish," and is related etymologically to the alimentary canal by which we digest food, and "aliment," which means "food."

"Alo" derives from Indo-European *al-, meaning "to grow, nourish," which, in suffixed form, is *al-to-, meaning "grown." From these Indo-European roots we derive such well-nourished and grown words as old, eldest, alto, adult, alumnus, haughty, and— by not nourishing—abolish. A bird born helpless, naked, and blind (certainly in need of nourishment) is "altricial," from Indo-European root *al- via Latin *altric-*, meaning "female nourisher." This same Indo-European root provides the source of such "grown" words as hautboy (a "high wood," commonly known as an oboe), altimeter, altitude, enhance, exalt, and coalesce.

amnesty | mnemonic

If you are unable to remember, you have amnesia, a word derived from the Greek word *mimnḗskesthai* (to recall), related to the Greek word that is the root of "mnemonic," and prefix *a-* (not). A "forgetting" or pardon for past offenses against a government is an amnesty. This word derives from related Latin *amnestia*, which in turn derives from Greek *amnestia*, meaning "oblivion." Amnesty, amnesia, and mnemonic all derive from Indo-European root *men-, meaning "to think," with derivatives referring to various qualities and states of mind. For other words based on *men-, see admonish/money and maniac/automatic.

Mnemosyne, daughter of Uranus and Gaea, was the Greek goddess of memory. Her daughters, fathered by Zeus, were the nine Muses, who inspired poets, musicians, artists, and others. In ancient Greece, a shrine to the Muses, a place of study, or library, was called a Mouseiôn. Today, we call such a place a museum. There is no link between the inspirational Muses and the word "muse" or "amuse," both of which derive from medieval Latin *musum,* meaning "animal's mouth." (Someone who muses or is amused may appear to be open-mouthed.) *Musum* is also the source of our word "muzzle," whether of an animal or a gun.

Mnemosyne's name is the Greek word for memory. In Greek, *mnemonikos* means "of or pertaining to memory." "Mneme" is the capacity of a sentient being to retain the aftereffects of experience or stimulation. A "mnemonic" device is a memory aid. For example, "Roy G. Biv" is a mnemonic to remember the order of the colors of the rainbow (red, orange, yellow, green, blue, indigo, violet).

In ancient Greece, *mousikè téchnē* (the art of the Muses) initially referred to any of the arts inspired by the Muses, then referred to poetry sung to music and, finally, to the music itself. *Mousikè* is the source of our word "music." In a similar tribute to the Muses, ancient Romans referred to decorative artwork comprised of inlaid pieces of stone, glass, and marble as *musaicum* (work of the Muses), source of our word "mosaic."

You don't require the powers of Mnemosyne to remember these mnemonics:

> The order of the planets: Most Volcanoes Erupt Moldy Jam Sandwiches Under Normal Pressure; My Very Excellent Memory Just Stores Up Nine Planets; Mary's Violet Eyes Make John Sit Up Nights (Period); or My Very Educated Mother Just Sent Us Nine Pizzas (for Mercury, Venus, Earth, Mars, Jupiter, Saturn, Uranus, Neptune, and Pluto).

> The biological classification of life-forms: Kings Play Cards On Fairly Good Soft Velvet; or King Philip Came Over From Germany Speedily (for kingdom, phylum, class, order, family, genus, species, and variety).

> The musical notes represented by the lines in the treble clef: the righteous Every Good Boy Deserves Food, or the perverse Every Good Boy Deserves Flogging (for E, G, B, D, and F).

Mnemonics have become useful for remembering telephone numbers (including numbers designed to spell words) and computer passwords. The most common computer password, ironically, is PASSWORD.

The first known password was not a mnemonic, though, but a word the enemy could not pronounce. In the biblical account of the war between the Gileadites and the Ephraimites (Judges 12:4–6), the routed Ephraimites attempted to cross the Jordan River at a ford held by the Gileadites. If someone denied being an Ephraimite, he was asked to say *shibboleth* (Hebrew, meaning "ear of corn" or "stream"). The meaning was not important, because it was the pronunciation that gave away the Ephraimites, who could not pronounce the "sh" sound. If the answer sounded like "sibboleth," the unfortunate soul was promptly stoned to death. Today, a shibboleth is a word or pronunciation that distinguishes people of one group or class from another, a catchword, or a slogan.

There are other examples of password shibboleths. In the thirteenth century, Sicilians who rose against the oppression of the French king were determined to kill all Frenchmen on Sicilian soil. Sicilians asked strangers to say *cecceri* (chickpeas). If the pronunciation sounded foreign, the stranger was killed on the spot. During World War II, American GIs tested suspected Japanese spies, who impersonated our Chinese allies, by asking them to pronounce words such as "mellifluous," "unintelligible," and "lollapalooza," which presented no problem for the Chinese, but which were very challenging to the Japanese. If the *l*s sounded like *r*s, the suspected spy was taken into custody.

ankle | English

The Indo-European root *ang- or *ank-, source of "ankle," meant "to bend." The ankle is, literally, a part of the leg that bends (just as "knee" derives from a different Indo-European root, also meaning "to bend"). Angle, also derived from *ang-, entered the language in the Old English period, and originally meant "fishing hook."

In the Jutland peninsula, in northern Germany, there is a fish-hook-shaped area that, because of its shape, was known as "Angul," and is now known as "Angeln." Those living there, known as "Angles," were the Germanic people who, with the Saxons and Jutes, crossed the North Sea to settle Britain about 1,500 years ago. The Angles settled to the north of the Saxons, along the east coast and in the Midlands. They gave their name to "England." By the time of the Norman Conquest, "English" applied not only to the Angles, but also to the combined West Germanic, Celtic, and Scandinavian population of England, as distinguished from the French or Normans. Within a generation or two after the Norman Conquest, even that distinction had disappeared.

Today, we apply "body English" by twisting our bodies in an illogical but irrepressible attempt to angle an already released ball to travel in the desired direction. "Body English" is the remote control version of the earlier use of "English," initially a billiards term, used to describe the angled spinning motion achieved by hitting a billiard ball off center. This use of "English" may derive from the name of the country of origin of an enterprising billiards player who impressed Americans in the nineteenth century with his ability to put this spin on the ball. (Ironically, English players call this technique "side," while "English" is only an American usage.) The earliest recorded use of "English" for this meaning is in Mark Twain's *Innocents Abroad* (1869): "You would infallibly put the 'English' on the wrong side of the ball."

asterisk | disaster

The Indo-European root *ster-, meaning "star," evolved into the Greek word *aster* and the Latin words *stella* and *astrum*. From the Latin we get our words "stellar" and "constellation" (literally, stars together). From the Greek we have the star-shaped aster flower,

astronomy, and astrology. "Asterisk" is from Greek *asterískos,* the diminutive of "aster," meaning "little star."*

Computer hacker's lingo for an asterisk reflects its astronomical origin: "star," "aster," and "twinkle." (Other synonyms are witty rather than astronomical, including "gear," "splat," "dingle," "mult," "spider," "glob," and "Nathan Hale," the last based on Hale's famous statement that "I regret that I have only one asterisk for my country!")

The derivation of "disaster" is based on an astrological concept. Combining the pejorative prefix *dis-* with *astrum,* the Italians

---

*As you see, the asterisk is a handy device to refer the reader to a footnote. It can also be used to denote Indo-European roots; qualify the main text, for example as formerly used in reference to Roger Maris's home run record (achieved during a season longer than Babe Ruth's); and direct the reader to the fine print (such as when the bold print advertises "zero percent financing" but the asterisked fine print informs you that you are not qualified for it). The asterisk takes on larger proportions, and greater meaning, in Garry B. Trudeau's comic strip *Doonesbury,* in which butterfly-ballot-benefited George W. Bush, who won the presidency only after the intervention of the U.S. Supreme Court, is depicted by nothing other than an asterisk.

developed *disastro* as a back formation from *disastrato*, literally "ill-starred." An occurrence supposedly resulting from malevolent astral influence is a disaster. When the word "disaster" was quite new in English, Shakespeare made eloquent use of it in *King Lear,* as Edmund rails: "We make guilty of our disasters the sun, the moon, and the stars . . . by an enforce'd obedience of planetary influences."

Related conceptually but not etymologically, Italian *influenza* has the same meaning as English cognate "influence." In the fifteenth century, Italians blamed sudden epidemics whose earthly causes were not apparent on the "influenza" of the stars. News of a Roman epidemic in 1743 brought the word to English. We now know enough about the causes of "flu" that, rather than blaming the stars, we get inoculations. (See inoculate/binoculars for more.)

Influenza is in the family of words derived from Indo-European root *bhleu-, meaning "swell, well up, overflow," with doublets bloat, fluid, flume, fluent, affluent, confluent, effluent, fluoride, influence, mellifluous, and superfluous. Based on astrological theory, the power of the stars wells up and overflows all the way to Earth, causing the hapless victim of that power to contract influenza. Thus, influenza and disaster share a core concept, that stars control our fate.

attorney | tournament

In Greek, *tórnos* referred to a lathe, a machine that holds wood or metal, rotating it for shaping. Latin borrowed the Greek word to make the verb *tornare,* to turn on a lathe. Old English in turn borrowed from the Latin for the verb *turnian,* meaning "to turn." Before 1200, this verb was shortened to *turnen,* and later, to *turn.*

In Old French, *atorner* meant "turn to," as in "to assign, appoint." The past participle of *atorner* was *atorné,* which, used as a noun, meant someone appointed to act as someone else's agent. Borrowed into English in the thirteenth century as "attourney," this word meant "acting for another by attorney." In Shakespeare's

Richard III, written about 1592, Richard requests the mother of the woman he loves to be his advocate—to "be the attorney of my love to her. Plead what I will be, not what I have been."

Over the centuries, "attorney" came to mean a lawyer practicing in the common law courts. The older sense survives today in the "attorney in fact," as contrasted with the "attorney at law." An attorney in fact is someone, not necessarily a lawyer, who has the power of attorney to act on behalf of—in turn for—another. Since clients turn to attorneys for advice and guidance and request them to act in their stead as their agents, it is most appropriate that these professionals are so named. Ambrose Bierce's ironic definition of "attorney" emphasizes the agency relationship between attorney and client: "a person legally appointed to mismanage one's affairs which one has not himself the skill to rightly mismanage."

The second *t* in "attorney" was an attempt to correct the spelling by Latinizing the form to what was thought to be its original Latin elements: *at,* variant of *ad,* meaning "toward," and *tornare,* meaning "turn."

The attorney's counterpart is the "client," a word derived from Latin *cluere,* meaning "listen, follow, obey." The present participle of this verb, *cluens,* developed an alternate form *cliens.* Someone who was *cliens* was always listening out for another's orders, rather than taking independent action. *Cliens* may be related to Latin *clinare,* meaning "to lean or bend," giving *cliens* the related sense of "one who leans on another." A client, etymologically speaking, is someone who leans on an attorney, to whom the client turns for advice and counsel. Other words related to *clinare* include lean, lien, incline, decline, recline, and proclivity.

The same Latin root that gave us attorney, *tornare,* is the source of "tournament," by way of Old French *torneiement* and medieval Latin *tornamentum,* based on the idea of "to joust, tilt." The medieval version of a tournament was a martial sport in which two groups of mounted and armored combatants fought against each other with blunted lances or swords. Today, the weapons of choice for tournaments are tennis racquets and chess pieces. The generalized sense of a contest in any game or sport in which competitors play a series of elimination rounds was first recorded in 1761.

Words related to "attorney" and "tournament" include return, detour, contour, tourney, and tourniquet and "tor" words, each with its own twist, such as torment, tornado, torque, torsion, tort (the wrongful act, not to be confused with torte, the dessert), tortuous, and torture. Less obviously related words, all from Indo-European root *terkw-, meaning "to twist," are extort, retort, thwart, torch (originally, twisted flax or hemp dipped in wax and then lit; now, for Brits, a flashlight), and possibly queer (from Middle Low German *dwer* and German *quer,* meaning "across, oblique, off center").

August | inaugurate

In 27 B.C., the senate granted Julius Caesar's great-nephew and successor, Gaius Octavianus, the honorary title Augustus, conveying the sense of "imperial majesty." The senate also honored Gaius Octavianus by changing the name of the sixth month, until then known as "Sextilis" (literally "sixth month," applicable when the year began in March) to "Augustus." Sextilis was the month in which Augustus became consul, conquered Egypt, put an end to civil wars, and achieved his greatest military triumphs.

This eponymous honor, which may have been at his prodding, presented Augustus with a problem. The senate had already renamed the fifth month "Julius," after his great-uncle. Julius's month had thirty-one days, while Augustus's month had only 30— a slight to Augustus. He cured this deficiency by taking a day from Februarius, named after a rite, not a person, and adding it to his month. This explains why February is the shortest month. For more about naming our months, see admonish/money and dean/December.

It is fitting that our word "august" means "inspiring reverence or admiration; of supreme dignity and grandeur; majestic; venerable; eminent." The reign of Augustus Caesar was a period of great progess and of a flowering of literature known eponymously as the Augustan Age.

The honorary term "august" originally meant "consecrated with favorable auguries." This sense derived from the augur, the ancient Roman religious official who advised government officials by foretelling events with auguries, or omens, based on observing the flights, songs, eating habits, and entrails of birds. A modern reference to this ancient form of soothsaying survives in the comment that an event does not "augur well" for the future, as in: "That storm cloud does not augur well for our picnic this afternoon."

No important enterprise was begun without consulting the augur to determine if the auguries were favorable. To consecrate or install someone in office when such omens were favorable was, in Latin, *inauguratio,* which gives us our "inauguration" of public officials, even though we perform that ceremony without the benefit of the examination of bird entrails.

The name "augur" comes from the Latin verb *augere* (to increase), because augurs enacted the symbolic increase or growth of crops. *Augere* is the source of augment, auction (for increasing bids), and nickname (literally, "an additional name," formerly spelled "an eke name"). This earlier "eke" form survives in our word "eke," as in "She eked out a living by working two jobs."

All these words derive from Indo-European root *aug-, meaning "to increase." Other words in this extended family are author, authorize, auxiliary, and the waxing of the moon ("wax" from Old English *weaxan,* meaning "to grow").

Ancient Roman culture survives in names of all our months, not just August. Ianus mensis (January) honored double-visaged Ianus (Janus), custodian of the universe, opener and fastener of all things, and source of our word "janitor." Februarius mensis (February) honored Februus, the personification of the rite of Lupercalia, which occurred that month. Lupercalia was a fertility rite, which included the sacrifice of goats and dogs. These sacrifices were known as *februalia.* The fact that we celebrate Valentine's Day each February may relate to this ancient rite.

Martius mensis (March) honored Mars, originally god of agriculture and forests, appropriate for the season of spring planting. Martius mensis was the first month for ancient Romans until 153 B.C., when January began the year. As mythology adapted to changing times, Mars became god of war as well as of agriculture. Our word "martial," as in "martial arts" and "martial law," is an eponymous tribute to Mars.

Aprilis mensis (April) honors Aprilis, the Roman counterpart to Greek Aphrodite, goddess of love, and source of our word "aphrodisiac." Maium mensis (May) honors Maia, Roman earth goddess of fertility. The remaining months, other than July and August, derive from the time when the Roman calendar began with March. Thus, September through December are named for Latin *septem, octo, novem,* and *decem* (seven through ten), even though these are now our ninth through twelfth months.

bagel | buxom

The Indo-European root *bheug- meant "to bend," whence we derive the bent "bow" that propels an arrow and the "bow" that acknowledges applause, by way of Old English *bugan.* If you stand with your hand on your hip with an elbow bent outward, your appearance is like that of a sharply bent "keen" bow—"akimbo"— via Middle English *kenebowe.* Your "elbow" bends at the joint. (The first syllable of "elbow" derives from Indo-European *el-, also meaning "bend," source of "ulna" for the forearm bone; thus "elbow" is the redundant "bend bend.") If you bend dough far enough to make a circle, you make a bagel, a word derived via Middle High German *boug,* meaning ring or bracelet, from the same Indo-European root. But what about "buxom"?

Old English *buxum* meant "obedient, someone who bends to the command of another," also from Old English *bugan,* to bend. This sense continued into the fourteenth century, as in William Langland's phrase from *Piers Plowman* "and buxom to the law," meaning submissive to it. Middle English variants *buhsaum, bow-som, buxum,* and *ibuscum* came to have a cluster of related meanings: obedient, humble, cheerful, patient, submissive, hardworking, robust, comely, healthily plump, and vigorous. By the sixteenth century, the term referred only to women, in the sense of a powerfully built working wench. In 1632, John Milton wrote a poem, "L'Allegro," in which he used "buxom" in the sense of lively and vivacious when he described Euphrosyne, goddess of mirth, as "buxom, blithe, and debonair."

balloon | ballot

The Indo-European root *bhel- meant to blow or swell, with derivatives referring to various round objects. Bowl, bulk, boulevard, bulwark, bull, ball, balloon, and, figuratively, bold and bawd, all derive from this root, as does ballot.

The Italian word *ballotta* means "small ball." Centuries ago, people voted by dropping small balls into a box or other receptacle, white in favor, and black against. (This voting process avoids any ambiguity created by butterfly ballots; swinging, hanging, and pregnant chads; and the like.) Today, if someone is not voted in, they are "blackballed."

The swelling sense of *bhel- also survives in "phallus," which must swell to perform its reproductive function, and in "fool." "Fool" derives from *bhel- via Latin *follis,* a bellows. In Late Vulgar Latin, *follis* came to mean a windbag, an empty-headed person—a fool. *Follis* is also the root of "follicle" (from its bulbous root in the scalp) and "full."

bankrupt | banquet

The Indo-European root *bheg- meant "to break." The bank of keys on a keyboard and the riverbank figuratively "break" the contour of

the area beneath. A bank of earth can be used as a bench. Medieval Italian moneylenders sat at benches or tables, called *banca*, source of our word "bank," for a place where money is kept. An insolvent Italian moneylender was symbolized by a broken bench—a *banca rotta*—figuratively, without the wherewithal to do business. *Banca rotta* evolved into our "bankrupt"—a person whose business is, figuratively, broken.

Less obviously related is "bunco, bunko," the swindle in which an unsuspecting person is cheated, as in a confidence game. "Bunco" derives from the same Italian word *banca,* and is probably an alteration of Spanish *banca,* a card game.

"Banquet" evolves from the same Indo-European root, via Italian *banchetto* (diminutive of *banco*) and Middle French *banquet,* meaning "little bench." Originally, a banquet was a small snack eaten while seated on a bench, rather than at a table. Over time, the meaning expanded, in reference to benches placed around a table, to mean "a feast."

belly | budget

"Belly" derives from Indo-European root *bheigh-, meaning "to swell." Words for other things that swell derived from this root are bellows, billowing, bulge, and bolster (whether the pillow or the act of buoying up another person or cause). Old English *baelg, belg,* and *bylg* meant "bag." The "belly" is a form of bag that holds the abdomen and bowels. With this sense in mind, by 1200, these Old English words had evolved to *beli,* meaning abdomen and bowels.

How did "budget" join this family of "swell" words? In ancient Rome, a *bulga* was a leather sack which, like a belly, is another form of bag. In Middle French it was called a *bougette,* evolving into English around 1425 as "bowgette," meaning small bag or wallet. From there, it was a small shift to its modern sense, meaning "the amount of money that is available for, required for, or assigned to a particular purpose." The modern sense of "budget" first appeared in 1733 with reference to the British chancellor of the exchequer presenting his annual statement.

berserk | hopscotch

"Berserk" derives from *berserkr,* the name of the followers of Woden, the chief god of the Anglo-Saxons and the leader of the wild hunt. Woden's name gives us the *d* in "Wednesday," reflecting our Anglo-Saxon heritage.

Berserkr derives from two Old English words: *bera,* meaning "light brown," and, by extension, "brown animal, bear," and *scyrte,* meaning "a short garment," from Indo-European *sker- or *skur-,* meaning "to cut." The *berserkrs* fought with frenzied ferocity, trusting Woden's power to protect them. They were dedicated warriors, devoting their lives to battle, and serving as bodyguards to heathen kings. In battle, they wore skins of bears and wolves, howled like beasts, and fought like wild animals. Our word "berserk," meaning "violently and destructively frenzied," embodies the spirit of these Anglo-Saxon warriors battling in their animal-skin shirts.

From the same Indo-European root, *sker- or *skur-, Middle English *scocchen* meant "to cut, score, gash." Our word "scotch," meaning "to put an end to, crush," derives from this word, as in: "The governor scotched all rumors about his interest in the presidency." "Hopscotch" derives from the scratching of lines in the dirt to make boxes for the game. Likewise, "butterscotch" developed in the mid-nineteenth century, so named because it was cut into squares. Thus, neither "hopscotch" nor "butterscotch" is related to the Scots, even though the alcoholic beverage "scotch" is.

Although the expression "get off scot-free" may suggest a link to the Scots, the term actually derives from another word in this etymological family, the *sceot,* or *scot,* a municipal tax in twelfth-century England. Someone who went "scot-free" succeeded in dodging this tax. The term "scot" evolved to mean "the amount one owed for entertainment, including drinks, in a tavern." Anyone who had a drink on the house went "scot-free." This term was reinforced by the fact that all drinks ordered in taverns were scotched, or marked on a slate, enabling a tavern keeper to make a reckoning of how much a person owed. (One theory is that "Mind your *P*s and *Q*s" derives from the importance of the tavern keeper tallying correctly the "pints" and "quarts" of drinks consumed, but that expression may instead be based on the care required of a typesetter to avoid mixing up these two similar-looking letters.)

Because of its utility, Indo-European root *sker- or *skur- produced many words. Cutting a robe "short" makes it into a "skirt," and cutting it even shorter makes it a "shirt." Other words related to *sker- and *skur- are shear (whether the shearing of sheep for wool or the wind shear when the wind cuts through the air), shears (we cut with), shearling (a sheep shorn once, and the wool cut from such a sheep), one's share (the cut-off portion), the plowshare (cuts into the earth), sharp (used to describe things that cut), shrub (rough vegetation), and the curt (short) reply. We also have a variety of related "sc-" words: the score of a game, which originally meant a score (record) scored (cut) on a tally stick; the music score; the scrape from being cut; the scraping process of scrubbing; scraps remaining after cutting; the scabbard, which protects a sharp sword; and skirmish, which originally referred to a fight with swords.

bid | Buddha

There are many forms of awareness, and ways to become aware. Indo-European root *bheudh- meant "to be aware, make aware." From Old English *beodan* (to proclaim), we derive our word for the process by which we inform an auctioneer of the amount offered: a bid. Something we are prohibited from being made aware of is forbidden, or verboten.

Old English *boda* was a messenger, and is the source of our word "bode," as in: "David's wild partying the night before his macroeconomics exam did not bode well for his getting on the dean's list." In Old Norse, an *unbodhsmadr* was a deputy. This word evolved, through Swedish, to our "ombudsman," the person who investigates complaints, makes findings, and mediates settlements.

The same root *bheudh- evolved, via Sanskrit *bodhati* (he awakes) and *bodhih* (perfect knowledge), to the name that Siddhartha Gautama, the Indian mystic, took once he achieved enlightenment: Buddha, the enlightened one.

brassiere | pretzel

The unifying concept for this unlikely doublet is the upper arm. The Greek word *brachýs* meant "short," with related word *brachíon*, referring to the shorter part of the arm—the upper arm. In Old French, *braciere* was a piece of armor protecting the arm. Over time, *braciere* was spelled *brassiere*, then shortened to *bras*. This word evolved to refer to the part of a woman's dress covering the body between the neck or shoulders and the waist. "Bra" was first recorded in English in the 1930s.

The same Greek word *brachýs* which is the source of "bra," evolved to Latin *bracchium,* meaning "arm," and *bracchiatus,* meaning "having branches resembling arms." Medieval Latin **brachitellum* was a kind of biscuit baked in the shape of folded arms. The name for this biscuit was shortened, via Old High German, to *brezitella,* German *Brezel* and *Bretzel,* and, finally, via modern German, to our "pretzel."

All these words ultimately derive from the same Indo-European root, **mregh-u-,* meaning "short." The "short part of the arm" sense survives from the same root in the "bracelet" worn on the arm, the "embrace" in which we put our arms around one another, and the "braces" men wear over their shoulders to keep their pants up, otherwise known as suspenders. (Extending beyond the torso, "braces" also refers to the dental appliance to correct irregular alignment of teeth.) In the singular, a "brace" (originally armor covering the arms) is a form of clamp; a device, such as a supporting beam, to hold something straight; an orthopedic appliance to hold something in the correct position; a protective pad strapped to the bow arm of an archer; and, in music, a vertical line connecting two or more staffs. The same Indo-European root evolved, via Latin *brevis,* to our words brief, abbreviate and abridge.

*Mregh-u-, via Germanic, takes on more philosophical meanings in words relating shortness to pleasantness. A person can shorten the apparent passage of time by amusing himself—and thus will be "merry," and even full of "mirth."

The etymology of "brassiere" has a striking absence of any reference to women's breasts which, of course, a bra supports. To this day, French women refer to a bra as *soutien gorge*, which literally means "throat supporter," although German women unabashedly call it what it is: a *Bustenhalter*.

Sex taboos have influenced language throughout history, and describing this garment without reference to breasts is just one example of linguistic prudery. English speakers in the seventeenth and eighteenth centuries altered their speech, so that "breast" became "bosom," "titbit" became "tidbit," "cockerel" became "rooster," "belly buttons" became "tummy buttons," and "underwear" was euphemistically abstracted to "unmentionables" and "small clothes" ("smalls" in modern Britspeak).

Of course, euphemisms extend to business and politics in a whole lexicon of sanitized speech, including, just by way of example: incursion for invasion, collateral damage for civilian casualties; pass away for die; pre-owned for used; budget for cheap; vintage for old; downsized for laid off; and, more literally sanitized than other euphemisms, sanitation worker for garbage collector.

broker | breakfast

Indo-European root *bhreg- meant "break." From it evolved Latin *broccus*, meaning "projecting, having projecting teeth," and Vulgar Latin *brocca*, referring to a pointed tool. Via Old French *broche* (a spit, awl, or pointed tool), this word evolved into Middle English as a verb, *brochen*, meaning "to pierce." This verb came to be used figuratively, as in "broaching" a new cask to dispense wine.

A person who tapped into casks was a retailer of wine—a wine broker. By the fourteenth century, via Anglo-Norman *brocour*, *abrocour*, a *brokour* was any commercial agent or middleman. This word is possibly akin to Spanish *alboroque*, the ceremonial gift at the conclusion of a business deal.

Related words from the same Indo-European root, all manifesting the sense of "break," are breach (a wall or a contract); the pointed-clasped brooch; and brioche, the flaky roll, which derives from *bhreg- via Old French *broyer, brier,* to knead. Less obviously based on the same root is "bracken," the weedy fern with large fronds forming dense thickets, which impedes, or breaks, motion when one tries to hike through it.

To broach the subject of a related set of words: *bhreg- evolved, via Latin *frangere, fract-* to many words conveying a sense of brokenness, including fraction, fracture, fragile, frail (breakable), fractious, infringe, refraction (breaking light into its component colors), and, less obviously, the song's refrain, which the singer breaks back into after each verse.

As unlikely as it may seem, the word "suffrage," the right to vote, also derives from the same *bhreg- root, via Latin *fragor,* meaning the noise of breaking, crash, din, or outbreak of shouts, as of approval by a crowd. In ancient Rome, the right to vote was known as *suffragium.* The "voice vote" is our modern counterpart.

One more word in the *bhreg- family is breakfast, the meal by which you "break" your overnight fast. The second syllable of "breakfast" derives from Indo-Euroean root *past-, meaning "solid, firm." The underlying notion, originally with reference to fasting as a religious duty, is that the period of holding firm from eating is ended by a meal. From this root we derive the words steadfast, avast (the nautical term, commanding sailors to stop what they are doing and stand firm), and the varied but related meanings of fast. "Fast" means resistent to destruction or fading (as in "fast colors"), lasting (as in "fast friends"), deep (as in "fast asleep"), moving quickly (as in "fast pace"), in quick succession (as in "the suggestions followed fast"), ahead of time (as in the watch that "runs fast"), and dissipated (as in "living fast").

"Fast" is one of those rare words that is its own antonym, in that "fast" colors remain in place and a steadfast person is firmly loyal, whereas a "fast" sprinter moves quickly. The clever name of a group of musicians devoted to writing at least one new folk song each week, combining both antonyms, is "Fast Folk." Other examples are "out" (Because of the power failure, all the lights went out. The moon came out from behind the clouds.); "sanction" (The women's lacrosse game was a sanctioned event. Sanctions were imposed for violating the rules.); and "oversight" (Government oversight of stock transactions helps prevent fraud. Because of his oversight, Henry forgot the apple pie for the picnic.). For another such word, see the discussion of "cleave" in hieroglyphics/clever.

buck | butcher

We hunt bucks, spend our hard-earned bucks (and sawbucks), pass the buck, buck each other up, buck the system, and are buck naked when we shower. This versatile word derives from Old English *bucca,* meaning "male goat," which, by 1375, in the form *bucke* developed a more generalized meaning of male deer, goat, or other animal. The verb "to buck" developed in the mid-nineteenth century, first with reference to the jumping of horses and mules with arched back and stiff legs, then figuratively to mean "fight against, resist stubbornly," as in the statement "You can't buck the system."

"Buck" for "dollar" has its roots either in trade or poker. In eighteenth-century America, a deerskin, commonly referred to as a "buck," was used as a unit of exchange, especially among Indians and frontiersmen. About 500,000 "bucks" were traded every year in eighteenth-century America. With its history as a form of currency, "buck" took on the meaning of "dollar" by the beginning of the nineteenth century.

In gambling establishments in the early West, a marker called a "buck" was placed next to a poker player to remind him that it was his turn to deal next, and face the unwelcome task of betting the next initial stake. That marker may have been a buckhorn-handled knife, or a buckshot, both readily accessible to frontiersmen. Over time, silver dollars were used as markers. Having the same function as these "buck" markers, these silver dollars, and by extension our paper money, came to be called "bucks." The uses of "buck" in both trade and poker may have reinforced each other.

A "sawbuck" for a ten-dollar bill is a nice confluence of "buck" for the jumping of an animal and "buck" for dollar. "Sawbuck" derives from two Dutch words: *zaag,* meaning "saw," and *bok,* originally meaning "male goat." It evolved figuratively to refer to a trestle or vaulting frame with X-shaped ends for holding wood to be sawed. In the 1850s, people observed the similarity between the Roman numeral X on ten-dollar bills and the X-shaped ends of a sawbuck. Even though our modern ten-dollar bills (actually notes) are stripped of their Roman numerals, they are still sawbucks.

The concept of "butcher" originally referred to a dealer in male goat flesh. From the same ultimate source as "buck," Old French *bochier* and Middle English *bocher* evolved more generally to mean a slaughterer of animals, and our "butcher." The figurative sense of a brutal murderer appeared in English as early as the fourteenth century.

bully | friar

Indo-European root *bhrāter- meant "brother" or "male," source of "brother" and, eventually, "bully." In Middle Dutch, *broeder* meant "brother," and Middle Dutch alteration *boele* meant "sweetheart, lover." In English, "bully" was a term of endearment, applied to both men and women, to mean "sweetheart" or "darling." Over time, "bully" retained its affectionate meaning but more generally came to apply to a good friend, and to any fine fellow. For example, in Shakespeare's play *The Merry Wives of Windsor,* written around 1600, when Sir John Falstaff enters the Garter Inn in act I, scene 3, the host greets him as "my bully-rook," "bully Hercules," and "bully Hector."

In the late seventeenth century, "bully" took on a pugnacious sense. A good friend or fine fellow can become rambunctious and was aptly described then as a "bully-huff" (a boaster who bullies) or a "bully roister" (a swaggering reveler). As of 1688, "bully" took on its present sense of a person who teases or hurts the weak. In Samuel Johnson's 1755 dictionary, he defined "bully" as "a noisy, blustering, quarrelling fellow: it is generally taken for a man that has only the appearance of courage." Noah Webster's 1828 dictionary similarly defines "bully" as "a noisy, blustering, overbearing fellow, more distinguished for insolence and empty menaces, than for courage, and disposed to provoke quarrels." For a similar deterioration in meaning known as pejoration, see cavalier/chivalrous and senator/senile.

"Bully" can also be used without pugnacity, as in "bully for you!" and Theodore Roosevelt's description of the presidency as a "bully pulpit." In this use, "bully" means excellent or splendid.

Other words derived from *bhrāter- came to us via Latin *frater,* meaning "brother": fraternal, fraternity, fratricide (killing a brother), and friar, a member of the Roman Catholic brotherhood. One final word in this brotherhood of words is "pal," from *pral*, with variants *plal* and *phral*, a word from Romany, the language of the Gypsies. This Romany word evolved from *bhrater- via Sanskrit *bhrata, bhratar-,* which means "brother." (The *l* in "pal" remains unaccounted for.) Gypsies speak Romany, an Indic language, because they originally migrated to Europe from the border region between Iran and India.

cadaver | cadence

Indo-European root *kad- meant "to fall." There are many literal and figurative ways to fall. After coursing down a "chute," water "cascades" down a waterfall. An "accident" is an unexpected event that befalls someone, possibly by "chance."

A "cadence" in music is the fall of the beat and, in cycling, the number of leg strokes per minute. The extended virtuosic section of a concerto for a soloist is the "cadenza." A "deciduous" tree (unlike coniferous trees, commonly known as evergreens) loses its leaves each fall, just as our deciduous baby teeth fall out, and a deer sheds its deciduous antlers. When land or property remains unclaimed, by "escheat" it reverts to the state, a legal concept dating back to the reversion of land held under feudal tenure to the manor in the absence of legal heirs or claimants.

The most protean word derived from *kad- is the utilitarian "case." It can mean occurrence (whether a case of mistaken identity or of the chicken pox), a lawsuit (the case of *Hadley v. Baxendale*), a set of reasons (present a good case for adopting a new national anthem), an eccentric person (a mental case), and the syntactic relationships among forms of a noun (nominative, genitive, dative, accusative, and ablative).

The ultimate fall is the falling of the body, by which each of our bodies becomes a "cadaver," which "decays" in the ground.

calendar | exclaim

In ancient Rome, the first days of each month were known as *calends,* derived from Latin **calere,* "to call out," cognate with Greek *kaleîn,* "to call." They were so named because in those days the pontifices (priests in charge of the calendar) publicly announced the first day of each new month and the order of days that would follow. Our word "calendar" derives from a Latin word, *calendarium,* a moneylender's account book, which listed the days of the month when payments were due.

The same **calere* root, and related Latin *clamare* meaning "call or cry out," give us clamor, claim, reclaim, exclaim, proclaim, acclaim, council (a calling together), and conciliation. Hearkening back to the monthly aspect of the calends, the name for the calendula, a plant of the daisy family, may derive from the fact that it was once used to cure menstrual disorders.

camera | comrade

You have probably taken a photo of a comrade with your camera, but how are the two related? "Camera" is pure Latin. It initially meant a "vaulted room," derived from Greek *kamárā* (vault, arch), which is related to our word "chimney." Over time, "camera" came to mean any room, and joined the lexicon via Old French *chamber.* This sense of "chamber" survives in the judge's "in camera" inspection of documents when an issue is raised about their disclosure to the opposing party or to the public. "In camera" review takes place in the judge's private study, known as "chambers."

The photographic camera is a miniature version of a chamber. In the seventeenth century, an optical instrument was invented that had the effect of a modern camera. It consisted of a closed box with a fixed lens on one side, producing an image of objects inside the box. It was called a "camera obscura," literally, a "dark chamber." When photography developed in the nineteenth century, "camera obscura" was shortened to "camera."

According to the iconoclastic theory of artist David Hockney, famous painters, all the way back to 1430, including van Eyck, Caravaggio, Titian, Raphael, and Velázquez, used projected images from a camera obscura directly to produce drawings and paintings. There is no question that certain artists used a "camera lucida" to create their masterpieces. A camera lucida is a small prism at the end of a rod, allowing an artist to see the face of a subject in the prism so the image can be sketched accurately.

In Spanish, the Latin word *camera* became *camara*. If a person stayed overnight at a public inn, he often roomed with others—known as *camarada*, meaning "roommates." This Spanish word crossed the border to France, where it became *camarade*. In Samuel Johnson's 1755 dictionary, he defined "camerade" as "one that lodges in the same chamber; a bosom companion." Our words "comrade" and "camaraderie" derive from the French *camarade*, as does the name for a car once manufactured by General Motors: the Camaro. From the same "camera" evolved "chambermate" and "chum."

canary | cynic

The derivation of "canine" is straightforward: Latin *canis*, and variant form *caninus*, mean "dog," from Indo-European root *kwon-, meaning "dog." Whether the canine in question is one of the four pointed teeth next to your incisors, the local K9 police squad, or faithful Fido, all derive from *canis*. And so does "canary."

In A.D. 77, Pliny the Elder published the first encyclopedia—thirty-seven volumes entitled *Natural History*. His encyclopedia recorded an account by Juba II (king of what is now Algeria and Morocco who lived from 46 B.C. to A.D. 19) of an expedition to a group of islands off the northwest coast of Africa, which found a roaming multitude of large dogs. Pliny named the islands "Canariae insulae," meaning "the Dog Islands."

Pliny's encyclopedia entry should be taken with a grain of salt. After all, Juba's expedition had taken place a century before Pliny put it on paper. So, whether dogs ever roamed the "Canariae insulae" remains a subject of speculation.

It is certain, however, that small green finches (*Serinus canarius*) *were* native to these islands. They were introduced as cage birds in England in the sixteenth century and were called "canary birds" because they were from the islands that had come to be known as the Canary Islands. The yellow domestic canary is a descendant of the wild green birds of these "dog" islands.

For the derivation of "cynic," we turn to followers of the fourth-century B.C. Greek philosopher Diogenes, who had contempt for sensual and intellectual pleasure, believing that virtue was the ultimate goal in life. Diogenes' followers acted in disregard of social customs and were known as *kynikos* (likewise derived from *kwon-), meaning "doglike"—either because of their conduct (which included sleeping in tubs) or because the gymnasium outside Athens where they held forth was called Kynósarges.

Today's "cynic" is their descendant, a term used since the sixteenth century to refer to a sneering, sarcastic person who doubts the sincerity of all human motives except self-interest. The association between cynics and dogs lasted at least through the eighteenth century. In 1634, Milton described cynics as foolish men "that . . . fetch their precepts from the Cynic tub, praising the lean and sallow Abstinence." Samuel Johnson's seminal 1755 dictionary includes this entry for "cynick": "A philosopher of the snarling or currish sort; a follower of Diogenes; a rude man; a snarler; a misanthrope."

Less obvious dog-based words are "chenille" and "cynosure." Chenille, a deep-pile fabric, derives from *canicula*, Latin for "little dog," via French *chenille*, which means "hairy caterpillar." The constellation *Cynosure*, also known as Ursa Minor, is of dog-related astronomical origin. This constellation, which contains the North Star useful for navigation, looks like a dog's tail. The Romans called this constellation Cynosura, from the earlier Greek *kynósoura*, a compound word from *kynós* (genitive of *kýōn*, meaning "dog"), and *ourá* (meaning "tail"). *Ourá* is also the source of "squirrel," whose tail is its predominant feature. (Words for some other animals are based on their dominant features. For example, "dodo" is a compound word from Dutch *dot*, tuft of feathers, and *ors*, tail, because it had a tuft of feathers on its tail; "reindeer" is a compound word from Old Norse *hreinn* and *dyr*, meaning "horned animal," and "lynx" is so named because of its shining eyes. For more on the derivation of "reindeer" see carrot/hornet, and for more on the derivation of "lynx" see lunatic/lynx.) In addition to its celestial meaning, a cynosure has come to mean anything that strongly attracts attention by its brilliance or interest (as in Milton's reference to a beauty as "the cynosure of neighbouring eyes"), or anything that serves for guidance or direction.

Our expression "dog days" for the hottest days of summer also has an astronomical source. In ancient Rome, the hottest weeks in the summer were known colloquially as *caniculares dies,* literally "days of the dog." During those weeks, Sirius (literally "scorching, burning"), the brightest star in the heavens, rises with the sun. Located in the constellation Canis Major, Sirius was also known as *canicula*, Latin for "small dog." According to Roman theory, Sirius added its heat to that of the sun. Thus, this period, roughly from July 2 to August 11, when Sirius's rise coincides with that of the sun, is known as the "dog days" of summer. The technical term to refer to these "dog days" is "canicular."

Other words based on Indo-European root *kwon- relate directly to dogs: corgi (from Welsh, *cor,* meaning dwarf, and *ci,* meaning dog, an appropriate word because of this dog's short legs), hound, and daschund. A daschund is so named because it was bred in Germany for hunting badgers, the German word for which is *Daschs.*

The derivation of "dog," first recorded in 1050, is somewhat of a mystery. It appeared in late Old English only once, as *dogca* (translating Latin *canis*), but did not appear again in recorded form until the thirteenth century. "Dog" has no known relatives of equal antiquity in other European languages, and is an early example of a native invented word, not borrowed from any other language. *Dogca* was first used for the name of a now unknown breed of powerful canines.

candelabra | candidate

"Candle" is one of the earliest English borrowings from Latin, probably arriving with Christianity at the end of the sixth century. The earliest record of this word is around 725, in *Beowulf*, as *candel*, although it appeared about twenty-five years earlier in the compound word *candeltwist*, with reference to an instrument to snuff candles. Latin *candela* derived from the Latin verb *candere*, meaning "be white, glow."

In ancient Rome, a person campaigning for public office wore a white toga rubbed with white chalk, to make it bright and spotless, symbolizing the unstained character of a person worthy of office. In Latin, the adjective for such a person was *candidatus*, from which we derive the word for our not-always-so-squeaky-clean political candidates. The same Latin verb *candere* evolved into our words candid, candor, incandescent, and candelabra.

All these words derive from Indo-European root *kand-, meaning "to shine." Other words from this root are incendiary, the verb incense (from Latin *incensus*, the past participle of *incendere*, to set on fire), and the noun incense, from the same Latin root. Incense does not produce its aromatic effect unless lit.

car | caricature

Indo-European root *kers- meant "to run." In Latin, *kers- evolved into *currere, curs-*, having the same meaning. A related Latin word, *carrus*, meant a wheeled vehicle, and evolved to "chariot," "carriage," and "car." In Latin, a two-wheeled vehicle was known as a *carpentum*. The person who made it was *artifex carpentarius*—our "carpenter."

"Caricature" is idiomatic. In Late Latin, "to load a wagon" was *carricare*. The related word *caricare* meant "to overload, exaggerate." This evolved into Italian as *caricatura* and French *caricature*. The earliest recorded use to mean a cartoon that ridiculously exaggerates a person or thing is found in Horace Walpole's letters of 1748.

A possible relative of the same Indo-European root *kers- is "horse." Semantically, the connection makes sense: a domesticated horse could pull a light cart or chariot at a run. Phonetically, although not obviously so, "horse" is related to *kers-. According to Grimm's law, a consistent *c* to *h* shift evolved from Indo-European to Germanic, a shift that did not occur in Latin. (Thus, we have such word pairs as cent/hundred, canine/hound, and cornet/horn. See the Introduction for more about Grimm's law.) By application of Grimm's law, the word "horse" may have derived from the earlier Latin *curs-* root.

Latin root *carrus* also passed into English as "career" (originally a road or racetrack and, by extension, the "course" of one's working life); "courier" (runner); "current" of electricity or water and "current" events that run with the times; "corridor" that runs down the hall; and the "cursor" that runs across the computer screen. A student who takes a "course" must follow the "curriculum," pure Latin meaning "race course." We "concur" (run with someone's opinion), "incur" (run into something, usually undesirable, as "to incur the wrath of a spurned lover"), and provide "succor" (run under, support). Events "occur" (run to meet us) and "recur" (run back).

Other words based on the same root are "discourse" (conversation running to and fro), "concourse" (gathering, or place for gathering), "cursive" (writtenwithlettersjoinedtogether), "discursive" (running from one subject to another), "excursion" (a short journey), "intercourse" (running between), "precursor" (forerunner), and "recourse" (what you run back to for help or protection).

"Curse" may be derived from the same Latin root *curs-*, via *cursus*, meaning "course." In the medieval church service, the daily liturgical prayers applied to "the set of imprecations," especially in "the grete curse," a formula read in churches four times a year setting forth the offenses that were cause for excommunication. Other possible sources of "curse" are the word "cross," Old French *coroz* (anger), or Old Irish *cursaigim* ("I scold"). But none of these has a meaning closely related to that of *curs* in Old English: formal sentence of excommunication, malediction, prayer, or wish that evil or harm befall another.

carnival | carnivore

The common element of both these words is flesh. Latin *caro, carn-* meant "cut-off flesh." "Carnival" is a compound word, from medieval Latin *carnelevamen,* a combination of *caro* (flesh) and *levamen,* a derivative of the verb *levare* (to lighten, remove, or raise). "Carnival" literally means "removal of meat." It first applied, in the form of *carnelevamen,* to the period of feasting and merrymaking preceding Lent, just before taking leave of meat eating. The most splendid example of such merrymaking is in the annual Carnaval in Brazil and other South American countries.

A carnivore is, literally, a flesh devourer, from *carnis* and *vorare* (to devour, also source of "voracious"). A carnivore devours meat dishes, such as chili con carne. "Carnivore" is patterned after the name Sir Francis Bacon applied in his 1627 publication of *Natural History* to a large order of flesh-eating mammals: "carnivora." "Carnivore" is also the code name the Federal Bureau of Investigation uses for its system to snoop on Web sites and e-mail, figuratively "devouring" everything it finds.

Words related to the same Latin root *caro, carn-* include carrion (dead and putrefying flesh), carnal (knowledge of the flesh), carnation (having flesh-colored blossoms), incarnation (reimbodiment in the flesh), carnage (massive slaughter; corpses of those killed in battle), and charnal (repository for bones or bodies of the dead). The carrion beetle and carrion crow feed on carrion, but the carrion flower merely smells like it.

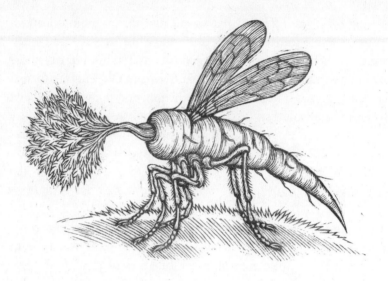

carrot | hornet

Indo-European root *ker- meant "head or horn," with derivatives referring to horned animals, horned-shaped objects, and projecting parts. The notion of "head" survives in our words cranium, cerebrum, cerebellum, and, less obviously, migraine. "Migraine" derives from Greek *hemikrania* (literally, half a head), because a severe migraine headache typically affects only one side of the head. "Cheer" is from Greek *kara* (head), via Old French *chiere* (face), and Middle English *chere* (expression, mood).

Names for animals with projections from their heads or from other body parts are members of this family of words: rhinoceros, triceratops, reindeer, unicorn, and hornet (think of its stinger). "Reindeer" is so named not for the reins on Santa's sleigh linking up Rudolph to Donner, Blitzen, and their buddies (that "rein" is from Latin r*etinere*, to retain), but instead is from Old Norse *hreinn* and *dyr*, meaning "horned animal." For a similar sense development by which animals are named based on their primary characteristic, see the derivation of "dodo" in canary/cynic, the derivation of "lynx" in lunatic/lynx, and the derivation of "salmon" in salacious/salmon.

For millenia, animal horns have been used as instruments, whence our words horn, alpenhorn, flügelhorn, French horn, and cornet. (In an orchestral score, the word for French horn, more akin to its Indo-European root, is "corno.") A horn can also be used as a container—thus our word "cornucopia," the horn of plenty.

Other words based on *ker- all relate to the concept of a projecting part: corn (on the toe, but not on the cob—that "corn" derives from an Indo-European root meaning "grain"); cornea (the outer coating of the eye); corner (the point to which two walls project), and its derivative, cater-corner (diagonal, out of line, or out of sorts); carrot (the root vegetable that projects into the ground); and, as unlikely as it may seem, carat. Carat, also spelled karat, the unit of weight used for precious gems, derives from Greek *keration*, the small carob seed used in ancient times as a weight for gems. These seeds grow in the horn-shaped pod of the carob tree.

cavalier | chivalrous

Here is a doublet of antonyms: cavalier (haughty and disdainful) and chivalrous (considerate and courteous). Both derive from the medieval Latin word for horseman, *caballarius*.

Historically, chivalrous conduct developed before a cavalier attitude set in. A derivative of medieval Latin *caballarius* was Old French *chivalerie*, the practice of riding horses. The earliest recorded use of this word in English was around 1300, in *Kyng Alisaunder*, to refer to a body of warriors or knights: "He schipeth into Libie, With al his faire chivalrie." Translation: "Immediately he embarks for Libya, with his entire retinue of splendid knights." Not long after that, chivalry took on the sense of bravery or prowess in war, a feat of knightly valor, or a gallant deed. In 1385, Chaucer wrote: "Whi hast thow don dispit to chiualrye? Whi hast thow don this lady vilanye?" Translation: "Why have you scorned the [ethical] code of chivalry? Why have you treated this lady so contemptuously?"

"Cavalier" evolved in the sixteenth century from the Latin *caballarius* via Italian *cavaliere*, then French *cavalier*. "Cavalier" initially referred to a courteous gentleman (usually one trained in arms), a mounted soldier, or even a knight. It was in the mid-seventeenth century that this term took on the surviving meaning "disdainful." For similar pejorative sense developments, see bully/friar and senator/senile.

In the sixteenth century, "cavalcade" meant a ride on horseback, and often applied to a military attack. By the seventeenth century, it developed the more generalized meaning of "procession on horseback." In this century, the "-cade" has been used as a suffix in its own right, in such terms as "motorcade," "aquacade," and even "camelcade." The "-cade" is actually from the last syllable of Italian *cavalcata*, a derivative of the verb *cavalcare*, "to ride on horseback." Other words derived from *caballarius* are caballero (in the American Southwest, a horseman, escort, or admirer), and chevalier (a member of certain orders of honor or merit).

chaise lounge | longitude

Chaise is French for "chair," derived from Old French *chaiere*, via Greek *kathédrā*, and Latin *cathedra*, a compound word combining *kata* (down) and *hédrā* (seat), and Latin *cathedra*. In England, "cathedra" meant "throne," especially a bishop's chair, located in the principal church of a diocese which, as a consequence, came to be called a "cathedral." This "throne" sense survives in such terms as the "chair" of the English department, a curious etymological development by which an honor is bestowed by turning a person into a piece of furniture.

Longue is French for "long." A *chaise longue* in French is a "long chair." As English speakers, however, we don't hear the "longue" as "long"—especially because of the way it is pronounced in French. We accordingly call it a "chaise lounge."

The word "long" (in distance and in yearning) derives from

Indo-European root *del- in its extended zero-grade form, *dlon-ghor (long), source of belong, linger, length, Lent (which may seem very long for those who abstain during this forty-day period of penitence from Ash Wednesday to Easter), longevity, lunge, oblong, prolong, and purloin (a fancy word meaning "to steal," literally, "to remove far away"). "Longitude," the reference to the location along the Earth's east-west axis, and its counterpart, "latitude," form a grid around the globe, useful in locating any spot on Earth. "Latitude" derives from Latin latus, meaning "wide." Ancient maps were marked with longitude and latitude, but with reference to a flat Earth—the length and width of a plane (consider the expression "to the four corners of the earth," a geometric possibility only in such a flat world). Today, we know that Earth is not flat, but we still gird Earth with these lines, and use longitude and latitude references for locating places on the globe.

"Chaise lounge" is an example of a type of borrowing from a foreign language known as Hobson-Jobson. A Hobson-Jobson word is an adaptation of a foreign word or phrase to fit the sound and spelling patterns of the borrowing language. Each April, Muslims of the Shia sect mourn the deaths of Muhammad's grandsons by chanting "Ya Hasan! Ya Husain!" To an English speaker, these words sounded like "Hobson-Jobson! Hobson-Jobson!" In 1886, Henry Yule, a member of the English occupation of India, published a book of Anglicized colloquial words from Indian languages. He titled it Hobson-Jobson.

Since so many of our words are formed by this process, "Hobson-Jobson" came to refer to any such borrowing. Here are some examples: "Juggernaut," originally referring to a cart, then to a very large and heavy vehicle, now refers to any relentless, crushing force or object. It derives from Sanskrit Jagannāth, a name for Hindu god Krishna. A cart honoring Krishna was drawn annually in a procession in eastern India. It is said that some devotees allowed themselves to be crushed under the wheels of this cart as a sacrifice to Krishna. "Mary Jane" and "Mary Jane Warner" are slang expressions for Mexican or Spanish "marijuana." "Taboo" (also spelled "tabu") derives from the

Polynesian language of Tonga, meaning "under prohibition." (The first written record of "taboo" is in Captain James Cook's 1777 journal while at the Friendly Islands, now known as Tonga.)

"Ketchup" derives from Malay *kēchap,* which was a sauce of fish brine, herbs, and spices. The name for this sauce reached Europe via sailors, who tasted *kēchap* and its variants, the ingredients of which depended on what was locally available. Those ingredients eventually included tomatoes, although in the eighteenth and nineteenth centuries the only common denominator was vinegar. Our word "ketchup" was first recorded in 1690 as "catchup," with later variants "ketchup" and "catsup," both of which survive today.

In Australia, "up the boo-eye" means "up the creek without a paddle," from the Maori word *puhoi,* meaning "slowly moving water, barely navigable"—an apt description of the Puhoi River, a small stream in the far north of Australia. "Plonk," a word for cheap wine, is from French *[vin] blanc.* In London's Hyde Park, you can ride your horse on a bridal path known as *Rotten Row,* so named because it is a corruption of French *Route du Roi* (Route of the King).

We need not look to foreign countries to discover Hobson-Jobson words, because numerous words derive from Native American languages, including Algonquian words from various tribes: chipmunk (*atchitamon,* meaning "one who descends trees headlong," probably Ojibwa), hominy (*rokehamen,* meaning "parched corn," probably Powhatan), moose (*moosu,* with reference to the animal's habit of stripping bark of young trees as food, probably Narragansett), raccoon (*arahkunem,* meaning "he scratches with the hands," probably Powhatan), skunk (*seganku,* probably Abnaki), caribou (*xalibu,* meaning "pawer, scratcher," with reference to the animal's habit of pawing snow to find grass, probably Micmac), hickory (*pockerchicory,* probably Powhatan), moccasin (*makisin,* probably Ojibwa), and possum and opossum (*apasum,* meaning "white animal," probably Powhatan).

We export as well as import Hobson-Jobson words. Despite the hard work of the French authorities, and laws enacted in 1977 making the use of Franglais a crime, French includes such intruders as *metingue* (meeting), *tiquet* (ticket), *roquette* (rocket), and *pique-nique* (picnic), not to mention the unaltered borrowings of such words as call girl, drugstore, and strip tease.

The Spanish version is "Spanglish," known in the American Southwest as Tex-Mex, Texican, or, pejoratively, as *español mocho* (from *mochar,* to cut limbs off trees). It includes such Hobson-Jobson words as *wachar* (watch), *pushar* (push), *bacuncliner* (vacuum cleaner), *fafu* (fast food), *microguey* (microwave), and *sanguiche* (sandwich).

Japanese, which gave us such words as kimono, karate, judo, tycoon, tsunami, rickshaw, bonsai, haiku, origami, judo, sushi, tempura, tofu, yen, futon, and zen, borrowed from English such Japlish words as *masukomi* (mass communications), *terebi* (television), *dokuta sutoppu* (a doctor's prohibition of certain activities), *yoguruto* (yogurt), *orenji jusu* (orange juice), and *sarariman* (salary man).

Here are more words in the Hobson-Jobsonized Japlish lexicon (all to be read aloud for full effect and all, of course, transliterated): *pasokon* (personal computer), *kado* (card), *teburu* (table), *burashi* (brush), *rajio* (radio), *eakon* (air conditioner), *dorai'ya* (dryer), *beddo* (bed), *bijinesu* (business), *shapen* (mechanical pencil, short for "sharp pencil"), *hoteru* (hotel), *rabu hoteru* (hotel for lovers), *kontakuto renzu* (contact lenses), *setah* (sweater), *baggu* (bag), *kapetto* (carpet), *sosu* (sauce), *basu* (bus), *baiku* (motorcycle), *toire* (toilet), *erebeta* (elevator), *biru* (building), *autoretto* (outlet stores), *konbini* (convenience stores), *depato* (department stores), *gorufu* (golf), and *tero* (terrorism).

The *sarariman* worked seventy-hour weeks of selfless loyalty to his employer. In a generational shift, millions of young Japanese, many of whom live at home, now reject such a harsh life, in favor of a more relaxed labor–leisure balance. These free spirits work when they like, and indulge themselves with foreign travel, hobbies, and whatever suits their fancy. They call themselves *freeters,* a borrowing from English "free" and German *arbeiter* (worker), an amalgam Hobson-Jobson word that could be described as Japgerlish.

In Cuba, a home run is a *honron*. In Germany, someone who is undecided is *wischiwaschi*. In Israel, the word for headlights is *sil-bim*, from the name of the American company that produced them, Sealed Beam. This name is fortuitous, since the plural form in Hebrew has the same "-eam" sound, and headlights come in pairs. In Brazil, English-derived words include *gilete* for a razor blade; *futebol* for soccer, with its *gols* and *penaltis; tennis* for any type of sneaker; *show* for a concert of popular Brazilian singers; *shopping* for a shopping mall; and *film* for a movie.

chameleon | human

A chameleon is, literally, a ground lion. Until the nineteenth century, this word was spelled "camelion," revealing its Greek root, *khamaileōn,* which is a compound of *khamaí* (on the ground) and *léōn* (lion). The Indo-European root of *khamaí* is *ghemo(n)- or *ghomo(n)-, meaning "earth." This root evolved, via Latin *humanus,* to our words human (earthling, in contrast to the heavenly gods), humane, humanism, humble (figuratively, close to the earth), and humiliation (which makes a person humble). Related Latin *humare,* meaning "to bury," is the source of "exhume"—to dig out of the ground. The same *ghomo(n)- root gives us homicide and *Homo sapiens,* but not homosexual, which is based on the Greek word for "same," as in homogenized, homogeneous, and homonym.

The word for the soil-enriching "humus," formed from decayed leaves and vegetable matter, also derives from this Indo-European root. Thus, human and humus share the same kernel idea, reflected in the biblical name of the first man, Adam, derived from the Hebrew word for earth, *adamah,* from which he was formed. The common root of "human" and "humus" gives an etymological perspective to the biblical idea of existence being "from ashes to ashes, dust to dust."

"Posthumous," meaning "occuring after one's death," owes its spelling, but not its etymology, to the word "humus." In Latin, *post* means "after." The superlative form of "post," meaning "last of all," is *postumus.* This word was applied to a child born after the death of his or her father. Since such a child was the very last that the father could conceive, the word "postumus" was associated with the notion of "period after death." This led to the perception of a link with *humus* (Latin for "ground") and *humare* (Latin for "bury"), and so in Latin "postumus" became *posthumus.*

Our English word "posthumus," initially referring to such a child and now more commonly referring to a book published after the death of the author, is based on the Latin, with the postburial sense intact. If the ancient Romans had had sperm banks, we might not have inherited this useful word.

champion | champagne

Pennant winners guzzling champagne after the final out may not realize it, but their postgame celebration is related etymologically to their on-field performance. Latin *campus* meant "field," or "flat ground," and survives today intact in the college "campus," and in the shortened form "camp," to refer to a good place for an army or other group of people to set up tents. A modern variant is to "camp" on a telephone line, a facility allowing an unsuccessful caller to be connected automatically once the receiving number is available—figuratively "setting up camp" on the line.

"Campus" came to refer specifically to the relatively flat ground well suited for battle, where there was room to maneuver. In medieval Latin, those who fought in such battles were called *campiones,* which evolved, via Old French, to *champion.* This original meaning survives in such expressions as "a champion of women's rights." The sense of "champion" as "winner" developed in the early nineteenth century in British English, and about the same time was shortened to "champ" in American English.

It was a famous battle that gave Champagne its name. In northeast France in A.D. 451, Roman general Aëtius defeated the Huns, repelling their invasion. This battle gave the name to this territory, whose rolling countryside, so conducive to battle, was also conducive to growing grapes. According to legend, about two hundred years ago the monk Dom Perignon invented the process of secondary fermentation in the bottle, using grapes from this region. The result: the bubbly that athletes and others, including politicians, imbibe to celebrate a successful "campaign," another word derived from the military sense of "campus."

clavicle | clef

In Latin, *clavis* referred to a key to unlock a door. In ancient Rome, to divorce was *claves adimere uxori*—literally, "to take the keys away from a wife." *Clavis* is the root for "clavicle," commonly known as the collarbone, because of its keylike shape. It is also the root for "clavichord," an early keyboard instrument, and for the musical term "clef."

A clef is the sign written at the beginning of a musical composition to indicate the pitch of the notes on the staff. It is, quite literally, the key to unlocking the pitches of all the notes to be played or sung. For example, the G clef indicates which line on the music ledger represents the note G.

The word "key" for a musical scale beginning on a given note (as in "the key of C") is not recorded before its use in Shakespeare's *Midsummer Night's Dream*, written in 1590. Originally, it may have been a translation of Latin *clavis* or French *clef,* after the musical system of eleventh-century monk Guido d'Arezzo, in which "clavis" meant a note or tone, especially the key note or tonic (the first note of the scale in which a composition is written). In his system, known as "solmization," d'Arezzo introduced the syllables "ut, re, mi, fa, sol, la" (from the Latin words of a hymn to St. John the Baptist) as names for the tones from C to A. This tonal system, with its characteristic key signature, has been the structural foundation of Western music since the Renaissance.

Although it may make sense conceptually for the key that operates a lock to be derived from the same Latin root, *clavis,* that "key" is ultimately of unknown origin, although it can be traced back to Old English *caeg.* It may be a cognate of Middle Low German *keie, keige,* meaning "lance, spear." Thus, even though the key to understanding "clef" is a Latin word for "key," our word "key," except in the musical sense, is unrelated to the word for an ancient Roman key. If you are not already hopelessly confused, consider the fact that, in French, the word for the key that unlocks a door is *clef* or *clé,* but the musician's key is *ton.* In French, *roman à clef* is a novel in which actual people, places, or events are depicted in fictional guise—reality being the key for this kind of fiction.

consider | desire

Even if you do not believe in astrology, you express a sense of being governed by the stars every time you consider something, or desire a certain result. Both words derive from Latin *sidus, sideris* meaning "star."

Astrology was a popular ancient Roman method of foretelling the future, which required carefully plotting the stars' courses. Latin *com-* is an intensive prefix, with variant form *con-;* thus, Latin *considerare* originally meant "examine the stars." Via Old French *considerer,* our word "consider" took on the expanded meaning of observe, and then, more figuratively, think over, have an opinion.

"Desire" is from Latin *desiderare,* literally "to await what the stars will bring," from the prepositional phrase *de sidere,* meaning "from a star." Figuratively, this word came to mean, from Old French *desirer,* "to long for or wish for something."

These words derive from Indo-European root *sweid-, meaning "to shine." From this same root, via Latin *sidus, sideris* and related word *sidereus,* meaning "starry," we have the word "sidereal," which means "of or pertaining to the stars." A sidereal day is the time required for a complete rotation of the earth, and a sidereal year is 365 days, 6 hours, 9 minutes, and 9.54 seconds (which is why we need leap years). A siderite is a form of meteorite containing nickel, and siderosis is a chronic inflammation of the lungs from inhaling dust containing iron.

court | horticulture

Indo-European root *gher- meant "grasp, enclose," with derivatives referring to an enclosure. Obvious words from this root include gird, girdle, and girth. Via Old English *geard* we have the enclosure we call a yard (grass in the United States, a paved area in Great Britain). *Gher- is also the source of "orchard" and "kindergarten."

In ancient Rome, a farmyard, or any enclosed yard, was called a *cohors*, a compound word, from *com-* (with) and *hortus* (garden, from *gher-). By extension, *cohors* came to refer to the people assembled in an enclosed yard, such as a crowd of attendants or company of soldiers. More specifically, *cohors* evolved to mean the sovereign's assembly, enclosures where kings and judges held forth, or a legal tribunal. Today's court of law (or tennis court, for that matter) was once a farmyard. The original sense survives in the first syllable of our word "horticulture," the science of cultivating plants. "Horticulture" is from Latin *hortus,* cognate with Greek *chórtos* (enclosed place, farmyard), and Irish *gort* (crop).

Cohors is the source of a family of words revealing various facets of life in the court, such as courtesy, curtsey, courteous, courtier, courtesan, and cortège. "Cortège" derives from Italian, *corteggio,* referring to a group of court followers, via French *cortège,* and now applies to a retinue, or to a ceremonial or funeral procession. "Curtilage" is a legal term for an enclosed area immediately surrounding a dwelling.

A "cohort," from Latin *cohortem* (accusative of *cohors*), originally referred to any group of people enclosed together. Jonathan Swift used "cohort" in the eighteenth century to refer to a group united in a common cause. The modern sense of "colleague" did not appear until the twentieth century.

*Gher-, in suffixed form *ghor-o-, is likely the source of such words as choir, choral, chorale, and chorus, all via Greek *chorós,* meaning dramatic chorus, dancing ground, and dance, and Latin *chorus,* meaning dance, band of dancers and singers. Terpsichore, muse of choral singing and dance, is the source of "terpsichore" (the art of dancing) and "terpsichorean" (related to dance). She derives her name from Greek *terpein* (delight) and *chorós* (dance). From *chorós* we also derive the name for the traditional round dance of Romania and Israel: the hora.

crisscross | cretin

In the fourteenth century, children learned the alphabet by writing it repeatedly on a hornbook. A hornbook was a primer of a single page protected by a transparent sheet of horn, and now refers to any rudimentary text. To gather courage for such a daunting task, children customarily made the mark of the cross, "Cros-Kryst," which stood for the phrase "Crist-cross me speed," meaning "May Christ's cross give me success." This formula was also said aloud before reciting the alphabet. By the sixteenth century, the alphabet row came to be called the "Christ-cross" row, eventually becoming "crisscross" row, and finally, in the nineteenth century, our word "crisscross" for any pattern having many crossing lines, or to move in such a manner. In the nineteenth century, "crisscross" was also the word for the game we know of as tick-tack-toe, and Brits know of as noughts and crosses.

At the end of writing the alphabet on a hornbook, and in old grammar books and primers, it was common for "&" to appear after *z*. When reciting the alphabet, children ended by saying after *z*, "and per se and," using the Latin *per se* to mean "by itself," a form that had been used in naming a letter that stood by itself as a word, such as *a* and *I*. We call it an "ampersand"—a contracted form of "and per se and." The character "&" is a stylistic writing of Latin *et*, meaning "and," invented by Marcus Tullius Tiro around 63 B.C., an early form of shorthand.

The name of Christ appears in "cretin" as well as "crisscross." A cretin, technically speaking, is a person suffering from a chronic disease due to a deficiency in normal thyroid secretion, character- ized by physical deformity, dwarfism, and idiocy. In the Middle Ages, some people living in the high Alps lacked sufficient iodine in their drinking water, causing a thyroid deficiency resulting in the medical condition we call cretinism. In the Swiss-French dialect of the Alps, these poor souls were called *chretiens*, or *creitins*, meaning "Christians." The underlying notion was that even such deformed and incompetent people were as much human beings as any other Christians, and should be treated accordingly. The word was adopted, via French *crétin*, as the clinical term. Human nature being what it is, "cretin" became a term of derision for a stupid or obtuse person. "Crisscross" and "cretin" are thus eponymous, both based on the name of Jesus Christ.

The euphemism "jiminy cricket" is also derived from "Jesus Christ." "Jiminy" is an alteration of Gemini, the name of the third sign of the zodiac, itself a euphemism for the Late Latin phrase *Jesu domine* ("Jesus Lord"). Thus, "jiminy cricket" is a euphemism for "Jesus Christ."

damask | damson

Damascus, now Syria's capital, was notable in the Middle Ages as a center for export to the West. This city, which may be the oldest continuously inhabited city in the world, derives its name from pre-Semitic "Dimashka," a name suggesting an origin before recorded history. Damascus was famous for its steel and its silk fabrics. "Damask" was the name Europeans gave to the elaborately patterned silk from Damascus, and "damascene" is an ornament made with inlaid gold or silver, or with a wavy design. That design was characteristic of the steel of swords made in Damascus, and of damask cloth.

The word for the small plum that we call a "damson" derives from Latin *prunum damascenum,* meaning "plum of Damascus." A fragrant pink rose, *Rosa damascena,* is known as the damask rose. Thus, one city gave us names for a fabric, a design, a fruit, and a flower.

We also imported eponymous words from Syria's neighbor, Turkey, including turkey, turquoise, and ottoman. Unlike "chicken," which originates from Old English *cicen,* recorded over a thousand years ago, "turkey" joined our lexicon only about five hundred years ago. The Portuguese imported the African guinea fowl to Europe through Turkish territory. Accordingly, this bird came to be called in England a "turkey" from its supposed place of origin, even though it was actually a native of Africa. When colonists from Britain settled in the New World, they found a wild bird that resembled the familiar guinea fowl (although the two are genetically unrelated), which they naturally referred to as a turkey.

You may choose to simplify this convoluted etymology of "turkey" by adopting the minority view of etymologists: "turkey" is a corruption of the Algonquian name for the bird, *furkee.* Of course, the Indian name may have enhanced the natural tendency of British settlers to apply the familiar and similar-sounding "turkey" to the apparently similar bird. But there is some poetic symmetry in misnaming a native bird for a place half a world away, since the colonists referred to the natives as "Indians" based on Columbus's mistaken notion that he had found the long-sought passage to India, also half a world away.

Like "turkey," "turquoise" derives from the name Turkey. This precious stone was first found in Turkestan and the Turkish dominions. This eponymous root is more obvious in Middle English *turkeis,* from the Old French *pierre turqueise,* literally "Turkish stone."

"Ottoman," the stuffed footstool, is named for Osman (also known as Othman), the thirteenth-century Muslim Turkish leader who founded the Ottoman Empire. In the eighteenth century, European merchants seized upon the popular interest in the Ottoman Empire by marketing items of luxury, including furniture, from the Middle East. This exotic furniture included a small backless couch for two that the French called the *ottoman.* Adapted in England in smaller form, it became the "ottoman footstool" and our "ottoman."

Place names are the sources of names for fabrics other than damask, and foods other than damsons. Other geographically eponymous fabrics include chambray (from Cambrai, France), calico (from Calcutta, India), and denim (from Nimes, via the French phrase "de Nimes") woven into jeans (from Genoa).

Geographically eponymous fruits and vegetables include brussels sprouts (from Brussels, Belgium), cantaloupe (from Cantalupo, a castle near Rome), casaba (from the Turkish town of Kasaba), cherries (from the ancient Greek city Kerasos), currants (from Corinth, via Anglo-French *raisins de Coraunte*), lima beans (from Lima, Peru), peach (from Latin *Persicum malum,* the "apple of Persia"), quince (from an ancient city in Crete, known as Cydonia), scallions and shallots (from Ascalon, a Philistine city in biblical times), and tangerine (from Tangier, the northern Moroccan seaport).

dean | December

Probably because we have ten fingers, we have a ten-based number-ing system and numerous ten-based words. Indo-European *dekm-, meaning "ten," became Greek *deka,* Latin *decem,* Old Saxon *tehan,* and *ten* in Old English.

A "dean" originally referred to a chief, first of ten men, then of ten monks, and finally, to the administrative head of a cathedral or college. "Dean" derives from Greek *dekanos,* Latin *decanus,* Old French *deien,* and Anglo-Norman *deen.* The same Old French *deien* evolved into our words "doyen" (male) and "doyenne" (female), elder or senior member of a group.

December means "tenth month," although it is the twelfth and last month of our year. The Roman calendar originally consisted of four months, all named for deities: Martius (month of Mars), Aprilis (month of Aprilis, also known as Aphrodite), Maius (month of Maia, earth goddess of spring and fertility), and Junius (month of Juno). Eventually, six months were added, named for their numerical order as the sixth through tenth months: Quintilis, Sextilis, September, Oct-ober, November, and December. Since this calendar was for an agrar-ian society, there was no need to mark time when fields were fallow.

Each month had thirty days, for a total year of three hundred days. The second king of Rome, Numa Pompilius, decided to account for these remaining days, and did so by adding after Decem-ber the months of Januarius, named for Janus (custodian of the universe, opener and fastener of all things, and source of "janitor"), and Februarius, named for *februa,* rites of purification. The date of the new moon just before the vernal equinox (which occurs in our March) remained the first day of the new year. Even though January became the first month in 153 B.C., our months September, October, November, and December still reflect a time when they were the sev-enth through tenth months. For further discussion of our names for months, see admonish/money and August/inaugurate.

An elaboration of the Indo-European root *dekm- was *dekm-tom-, meaning "ten tens." Via Germanic, this root evolved into "hundred." An even greater amount was the *tus- (strong or swelled) hundred, an amount we now call a "thousand." From the same root, the Latin equivalent of hundred, *centum* (which was pronounced with a hard *c*, as in "candy") is the source of century, cent, and percent, the number per hundred. Obvious descendents from Greek and Latin are decade, decagon, decimal, decibel (one-tenth of a Bell, a unit of sound named after Alexander Graham Bell), decimate (originally execution of one person in ten), decennial, Decalogue (the Ten Commandments), dime, and decapod (a ten-legged creature, such as the crab, the lobster, and the shrimp). From the Germanic we derive ten, the teens (e.g., thirteen is, literally, three plus ten), and one of the more benign words for those aged eleven to nineteen: teenagers. Less obvious descendents are dozen (from Latin *duodecim,* two plus ten) and dicker.

Dicker, while of uncertain origin, may derive from Latin *decuria,* parcel of ten, doublet of *decem.* More specifically, Caesar's legions used as a unit of trade in Britain and elsewhere a bundle of ten animal hides. The word for this trading unit was *dicor* in Old English, evolving to *dikor* in Middle English. American frontiersmen haggling over the price of ten pelts dickered over the price of a dicker. The word "dicker" was first recorded in modern English with reference to haggling while horse trading. In 1848, James Fenimore Cooper used "dicker" in the context of frontier trade.

dentist | dandelion

The word "dentist" dates from 1759, borrowed from French *dentiste,* which derived from Latin *dens, dentis,* referring to the tooth. "Dentistry" didn't enter the written language until 1838, and "denture" didn't make its appearance until 1874.

If you ever put your head inside a lion's mouth, you might notice the similarity of lion's teeth to the leaf of the weedy plant, *Taraxacum officinale,* commonly referred to as the dandelion. In Latin, this plant was known as *dens leonis* ("lion's tooth"), alluding to its serrated

lion-tooth-shaped leaves. In Middle French, *dens leonis* was translated as *dent de lion*, and entered English in the fourteenth century as "daundelyon" and "dent-de-lyon," then evolving to "dandelyon" in the fifteenth century. Other words from the same root (ultimately from Indo-European *dent-, meaning "tooth") are the three-toothed trident, indented (literally, toothed, or tooth-marked), tooth, and tusk (originally a canine tooth, as of a wild boar). The microscopic toothlike scales providing a protective layer on a shark's skin are "denticles." Like teeth, they are pointed, covered in enamel, and contain nerve—and, like a shark's teeth, they grow again, so the shark can terrorize other forms of marine life, and people, another day.

A less obvious "dent" word is "indenture," a legal term for a written agreement (giving rise to the term "indentured servant") or a deed. Historically, an indenture was written twice on a single sheet, which was then cut in half along an irregular zigzag indented line. By matching the notched edges of the two originals, like interlocking puzzle pieces, the genuineness of either could be proven.

dextrose | ambidextrous

Dextrose is a form of glucose through which the plane of polarization of light is rotated toward the right. This fact is biologically significant, since the process by which dextrose is converted into energy in the body differs from that of similar forms of sugar, which rotate the plane of polarization to the left. The "-ose" in "dextrose" is merely a chemical suffix referring to a sugar, found in words such as cellulose, fructose, lactose, and glucose.

Indo-European root *deks-, meaning "right side," evolved into Latin as *dexter,* meaning "on the right, favorable, skillful" and, via Old French, into our words dexterity, dexterous, and ambidextrous— literally, having two right hands. Ambrose Bierce defined "ambidextrous" quite literally, with an ironic twist, as "able to pick with equal skill a right-hand pocket or a left." Theodor S. Geisel, better known by his pen name, Dr. Seuss, nicely combines "dexterous" and "right" in *Oh, the Places You'll Go!*: "Just never forget to be dexterous and deft. And *never* mix up your right foot with your left."

Any right-minded person must be cognizant of the bias favoring right-handers implicit in the word "ambidextrous," especially when contrasted with the expression "two left feet." This bias is not always obvious, although it is apparent in such words as righteous, rightful, right-hand man, right (correct), all right, dead to rights, and the Bill of Rights. (There is, after all, no Bill of Lefts.) These words are not, however, related etymologically to the *deks- words. They stem from Old English *riht,* meaning good, fair, just, proper, fitting, straight, lawful, true, and genuine. "Righteous" derives from Old English *rihtwis,* from *riht* and *wis,* meaning "wise."

The root of Old English *riht* is Indo-European *reg-, which meant "to move in a straight line, lead, rule," with many related senses, producing various "rec" words. The *rec*tor, who lives in the *rec*tory, preaches *rec*titude to his parishoners, to di*rec*t them in the cor*rec*t way of living, and to *rec*tify any *rec*klessness. Other words from this same root, each conveying a "straight" sense in its own right, are erect (straight up), rectum (the straight part of the lower bowel), rack, rake (for the straight cross bar), rectangle (made of four right-angled straight lines), reckon (from Old English *gerecenian,* to arrange in order, recount), director, and directory.

This same Indo-European root evolved into Sanskrit *rājā,* meaning king, and our words raj, rajah, and maharajah; Latin *rex, regis-,* meaning "king," and our words regal, reign, royal, regicide, viceroy, and the Brazilian currency, the real; Latin *regula,* meaning straight piece of wood, and our words rail, regular, regulate, and rule; Latin *rogare,* meaning to ask, based on the idea of stretching out the hand, and our words interrogate, prerogative, derogate, abrogate, subrogate, and arrogate; and Greek *oregein,* meaning "to stretch out, reach out for." "Anorexia," loss of appetite, and anorexia nervosa, the psychophysiological disorder characterized by fear of becoming obese, derive from Greek *a,* meaning "without," and *orexis,* meaning "appetite."

There is nothing "straight" about the pejorative "left" words. In ancient Rome, *sinister* meant "on the left side" and its doublet, *sinistrum,* meant "evil, unlucky, inauspicious." All of these meanings survive today in our word "sinister."

The underlying concept was that omens observed from one's left were considered unlucky. To this day, superstitious people toss salt over their left shoulders. This denigration of leftness was a carryover from the Greek practice of predicting the future, in which the augur faced north when observing omens. When taking auspices, the east was considered to be the fortunate quarter. When facing north, east is to the right, and its opposite is to the left.

"Maladroit," our word for awkward, bungling, inept, and tactless, literally means "badly from the right," in contrast to its antonym, "adroit," which literally means "from the right." Less obvious is the attack on lefties hidden in the word "awkward." In Middle English, *awk* meant "the wrong way around, backhanded, from the left." Thus, a backhanded blow with a sword, even if skillful, was an "awkward" stroke (the second syllable evident in such words as "backward," "forward," and "toward"). The sense of "clumsy" is recorded as early as the sixteenth century.

The very word "left" is pejorative, derived from Old English *lyftl*, meaning "weak, lame." In Old English, the word for "paralysis" was *lyftadle*—"left-disease." This long-standing prejudice apparently reflects the fact that most people, ever since recorded history, have been right-handed.

Consider yet one more slam on lefties: gauche. This is pure French for "left," derived from Old French *gaucher, gauchier*, meaning "trample, reel, walk clumsily," and Middle French *gauchir*, meaning "turn aside, swerve." Today, "gauche" has taken on a figurative meaning, referring to someone lacking social graces, crude, tactless, and awkward.

"Left-handed compliment," the thinly disguised insult, probably derives from the now obsolete European custom that in the marriage ceremony between royalty and a commoner the groom gave his bride his left hand rather than his right. This symbolized the fact that in such a marriage neither the commoner nor her children would have any claim to her royal husband's property. Although the expressions "left-handed marriage" (any marriage to a socially inferior woman) and "left-handed wife" (a concubine) no longer survive, the more utilitarian "left-handed compliment" remains accessible whenever we hear a subtle put-down.

dollar | Neanderthal

Early in the sixteenth century, Count Stefan of Schlick minted a silver coin in the little mining town of Sankt Joachimsthal in northwestern Bohemia. Count Stefan's coins were 93 percent silver, and because of the rich lode in his silver mine, the count was able to mint a large quantity of coins.

The obverse (heads side) of this coin featured St. Joachim (St. Joseph) with the crest of the Schlick family. Because of the depiction of St. Joachim, and the place of minting, the obvious name for such coins was "Joachimsthalers." But that name was too cumbersome, and was soon shortened to *thalers*. The *-thal* in "Sankt Joachim-

sthal" means "valley." The town's name means "the valley of St. Joseph." The shortened term for the currency referred to the valley without its namesake.

In some German dialects and in the speech of the Low Countries, *thaler* became *daler*. By 1581, the word "daler" entered English as "dollar," referencing not Joachimsthalers, but the common currency of the time, the Spanish peso, which was patterned after the Joachimsthalers.

By the time of the American Revolution, the Spanish peso was widely circulated in North America, especially in areas dominated by Spain, and in areas involved in trade with the West Indies. The newly independent American government needed a name for its basic monetary unit, and the British "pound" just would not suit the revolutionaries. So it was natural to pick the familiar "dollar" for the unit of currency. The Continental Congress passed a resolution in July, 1785, that "the money unit of the United States of America be one dollar."

The same valley word *-thal* and English variant "-dale" appear in a variety of eponymous words referencing geographical origins. The cheese from Switzerland's Emma Valley is "Emmenthaler cheese." A dog bred in the valley of the Aire River in Yorkshire, England, is an

"Airedale terrier." Horses bred in the valley of the Clyde River in Scotland are "Clydesdale horses." And our early human ancestor, whose fossils were discovered in a gorge in the Neander Valley near Düsseldorf, Germany, is the "Neanderthal" man. Today, "Neanderthal" refers to any heavily built, crude, and dull-witted person.

A person's last name ending "-thal" or "-dale" may reveal the place of ancestry, or may be an adopted name. In the first half of the nineteenth century, Prussia, Bavaria, and the Russian Empire emancipated the Jews, but made their emancipation conditional upon the adoption of family names. Those names were subject to approval by the authorities, providing a means for governmental officials to extort money. Those who could not afford to pay were stuck with such names, for example, as Schmalz (grease), Borgenicht (do not borrow), Ochsenschwantz (oxtail), Galgenstrick (gallows rope), and Eselkopf (donkey's head). But people who could afford fine-sounding names, which came at a high price, had the benefit of names derived, for example, from gems, such as Diament, Edelstein, and Saphir, and from flowers that grow in valleys, such as Blumenthal, Rosenthal, and Lilienthal.

dubious | doublets

Two-ness is a versatile concept, expressed in Indo-European root *dwo-, which evolved into Latin as *duo,* and our words duet, duplicate, duplex, doubloon, duplicity, double, deuce, and dozen (this last word from Latin *duodecim,* literally "two and ten").

A person of two minds about something is in doubt or dubious. "Dubious" entered the lexicon in the sixteenth century, meaning "objectively doubtful; fraught with doubt or uncertainty; uncertain; undetermined; indistinct, ambiguous, vague." Its earliest recorded usage was in 1548: "To abide the fortune of battayle, which is ever dubious and uncertayne," In the seventeenth century, Milton used this word in a similar sense in *Paradise Lost:* "His utmost power . . . oppos'd /In dubious Battel on the Plains of Heav'n."

By then, "dubious" also came to mean "subjectively doubtful; wavering or fluctuating in opinion; hesitating," as in this quotation from 1632: "Though I beleeve . . . yet am I somewhat dubious in beleeving." By the nineteenth century, "dubious" also came to mean "of questionable or suspected character," as in this provocative quotation from 1884: "She had been absent from England . . . oftentimes in very dubious company."

In Old French, the wavering between possibilities took on a sense of "fear," which survives in our word "redoubtable" (literally, "fearable"), meaning arousing fear, awe, or respect. A fact too apparent to be doubted so as to be beyond question is "indubitable."

To etymologists, the word "doublet," the concept that inspired this book, refers to two or more words derived from one source. Versatile "doublet" is a handy word for anything doubled. It first appeared in the fourteenth century with reference to the close-fitting body garment, with or without sleeves, worn by men from the fourteenth to the eighteenth centuries, the prototype for the modern coat and jacket. This garment, which included linings, interlinings, padding, and stiffening, originated in military dress as a padded front over armor. By the fifteenth century, "doublet" also referred to the same number turning up on both dice at a throw, and to a counterfeit jewel composed of two pieces of crystal or glass cemented together with a layer of color between them. The seventeenth century brought "stone doublet" for a prison, presumably for its doubly thick walls. By the nineteenth century, "doublet" expanded in usage, to refer variously to the combination of two simple lenses, two birds killed at once with a double-barreled gun, a double-impact shot in billiards, two words derived from the same source, and the pair of words at either end of a word ladder. (An example of such a word ladder is the transformation of antonyms from head to tail via heal, teal, tell, and tall.)

The same Indo-European root evolved into "two"-based words, including the more obvious two, twelve, twenty, between, twin, and twice, and the less obvious twig (a forked stick), twilight (halfway between daylight and darkness), twist (turning left and right simultaneously), twine (originally, two interwoven strands), intertwine (to join by twining together), twill (woven of double thread), and twinkle (alternating on and off).

In the fifteenth century, "deuce" referred to a two-spot in the game of dice, then to a throw in dice which turns up as a two, the lowest and unluckiest throw. The mild oath "deuce" was the word gamblers supposedly cried out in disgust when they threw a deuce, possibly influenced by Low German *duus* meaning "the devil!" The tennis term "deuce," which dates back to the sixteenth century, refers to the fact that each team needs two consecutive points to win a game, and derives from the French *à deux de jeu*.

Many other words derive from Indo-European *dwo-, including biscuit and zweiback (both, literally, "twice-baked"), and numerous "bi-" words, such as binary, bipolar, bicentennial, bicarbonate, and combine; "di-" words, such as dioxin and dichotomy; and "be-" words, such as betwixt and between. Less obvious members of this "two" family are balance (from Vulgar Latin *bilancia,* meaning "a scale having two shallow pans"), and diploma (pure Greek, meaning a folded paper or document, from Greek *diplos,* meaning "double"), and related words diplomat and diplomatic.

endorse | do-si-do

When you write your name on the back of a check, or support a certain viewpoint, you endorse it. When you publicly back a candidate for public office, you endorse that candidate, and give your endorsement. Latin *dorsum,* meaning "back," evolved into medieval Latin *indorsare,* meaning "write on the back."

The meaning of "endorse" broadened over time. As of the fourteenth century, it referred to inscribing a document on the back with words indicating the nature of its contents, one's opinion of its value, or some extension or limitation of its provisions, and to signing one's name on the back of a check. By the seventeenth century, "endorse" took on the now obsolete meaning of sitting or loading something on the back of an animal, and the figurative meaning

common today—to confirm, sanction, countenance or vouch for statements, opinions, or acts of another—literally, lending support by "backing up" such statements, opinions, and acts.

Other words related to Latin *dorsum* include the dorsal fin on the back of a fish (such as a shark), the dossier consisting of a bundle of papers with a label on the back, and the British slang term "doss," to sleep or lie down in any convenient place, or a cheap lodging house.

"Do-si-do," the square dance call, instructs partners to circle back to back. It derives from French *dos-à-dos,* meaning "back to back." In Louisiana Cajun country, dancers *fais do-do* to zydeco. "Zydeco," the popular music of southern Louisiana combining French dance melodies, elements of Caribbean music, and the blues, derives its name from an alteration of the first two words of a song title: *Les haricots (sont pas salé)* meaning "The beans are not salted." (Sound, not sense, matters here.)

enthusiasm | theology

The word "enthusiasm" derives from Greek *enthousiasmós*, meaning "inspiration or possession by a god." This compound Greek word is based on *theós*, meaning "god," source of such words as "theology" and "atheist."

When the Greek noun was borrowed into seventeenth-century English, it retained the Greek sense. In the age of Puritanism, however, "enthusiasm" took on the derogatory connotation of "excessive religious emotion," and by the eighteenth century came to mean "zeal for a cause or subject."

"Theology" itself derives from compound Greek word *theologíā*, an account of the gods, or of God. The first element, *theós*, also appears in such words as "theosophy," a religious philosophy of the soul based on mystical insight into the nature of God, and "apotheosis," exaltation to divine rank or stature, deification, and, to a lesser extreme, an exalted or glorified example, as in the statement: "Their leader was an apotheosis of courage." The second element, *-logy*, from Greek *-logíā*, means the study or science of, as in the words biology, astrology, and philology, and, more generally, means speech, discussion, or collection, as in the words tautology, eulogy, and anthology.

These words derive from Indo-European *dhēs-, a root of uncertain religious meaning. Various words from this same root, via Latin *festa* (referring to religious holidays), are festival, fair, fiesta, feast, and festive, and via Latin *fanum* (meaning temple), the religious fanatic and the profane language used only outside the temple. Of course, with sports being a form of modern religion, we now have the sports fan whose very happiness depends on whether his team wins the big game.

feather | hippopotamus

This most unlikely word pair has its common root in Indo-European *pet-, meaning "to rush, fly," with suffixed forms

*pet-rā- and *pet-nā. "Feather" derives from Greek *pterón* (feather, wing). This Greek root is more obvious in the word for the lizard-like bird from the Jurassic period, the transitional form between reptiles and birds: the archaeopteryx. Latin *penna* and *pinna* (feather, wing), and Late Latin *pinnaculum*, diminutive of the same word, are the source of "pen" (think of the original quill pens), "penne" pasta (for its shape like the nib of a pen), "pinnacle," and "panache," this last word via Italian *pinnacchio* (plume), and Middle French *pennache* (plume and verve). The first use of "panache" in the figurative sense of "swagger, verve, flamboyance" appears in an 1898 translation of Edmund Rostand's *Cyrano de Bergerac*, although the use of "panache" for the ornamental tuft or plume of feathers adorning a helmet or hat was first recorded in English in 1819. A feather in one's cap is certainly an apt emblem for panache.

The "rushing" sense of *pet- appears in such words as petulant, impetus, perpetual, compete, repeat, and, most appropriately for anyone who has ever tried to diet, appetite. Latin *appetitus* meant strong desire, from *appetere,* to strive after. "Propitious," meaning favorable or gracious, is from Latin *propitius,* a religious term meaning rushing forward, eager, or well disposed.

Of course, when you rush, you sometimes fall. *Pet- evolved, via Greek *piptein* (to fall), *sympiptein* (to befall, coincide), and *symptoma* (accident, disease, a happening), to our word "symptom." "Symptom" first appeared in writing in 1541 as an indication or evidence of sickness.

So how does the massive, slow-moving hippopotamus, which has absolutely no sense of panache, and certainly can't fly, join this family of rushing and flying words? The answer is not in the "hippo" but in the rushing water where it thrives. Greek *potamós* means "river," originally "rushing water." Greek *híppos* means "horse." Literally, a hippopotamus is a "horse in rushing water." Hippos rarely wander far from water, where they feed on water plants and shore vegetation, feel buoyant, and stay cool.

flamingo | flamenco

As unlikely as it may seem, these two words are probably derived from the Flemings of the Low Countries. The link is in the color. The people of Flanders, Belgium, known as Flemings, were renowned for their lively personalities, flushed complexions, and love for bright-colored clothing, reflected in their portraits by such Dutch painters as Frans Hals.

When Spaniards came into contact with the Flemish Dutch, whom they referred to as "Flamenco," they were impressed by the pinkish Dutch complexion. As early as 1330, Spanish *flamenca* meant "of a ruddy complexion, flesh-colored." The Spanish word for the bird of a hue reminiscent of the Flemings was *flamengo,* and our "flamingo." An alternative etymology is that the bird's name derives from Latin *flamma,* meaning "flame," via Old Provencal *flamenc.* When a flamingo takes flight, the flash of its scarlet wing can be analogized to a burst of flame.

"Flamenco," the word for the provocative Gypsy dance from Andalusia, Spain, has the same eponymous source: the Gypsy's bright-colored clothing reminded Spaniards of the flamboyant Flemish attire, and they associated the fine appearance of the dancers with the healthy and ruddy complexion of the Flemings.

Some etymologists believe that the link between the Flemings and Gypsies has a darker side. In the early sixteenth century, King Charles I of Spain had several Flemish ministers who were unpopular with the king's subjects. Accordingly, "Flamenco," the Spanish word for "Fleming," became a disparaging term for any foreigner. According to this theory, when Gypsies migrated to southern Spain in the sixteenth century, Andalusians applied this term to them in derision. The name for the Gypsies stuck and survives to this day to describe their unique dance.

Prejudice against Gypsies also survives in the word "gyp," meaning "to cheat, swindle." In the sixteenth century, members of a race of people of Hindu origin, who called themselves and their language "Romany," began to settle in Britain. The British, incorrectly believing the Romany to be from Egypt, called them "Egipcyans," soon shortened to "Gipcyan." By 1600, variants included "Gipsy" and "Gypsey." The earliest recorded example is in Shakespeare's *As You Like It,* in reference to two pages singing a song "both in a tune, like two gipsies on a horse." The word "gypsy" has also been applied to women, both contemptuously and playfully. A prime example is the stage name of ecdysiast Rose Louise Hovick: Gypsy Rose Lee.

The French thought the Romany were from Bohemia, and accordingly called them "Bohèmes," source of our word "bohemian," referring to someone living with disregard for conventional rules of behavior.

As early as the seventeenth century, "gypsy" was used in a figurative sense to mean "a cunning rogue," of whatever ethnicity. The nineteenth century brought "gyp" to American slang, the verb form of the noun. According to the *Oxford English Dictionary,* however, "gyp" may derive from "gippo," later shortened to "gyp," referring to the short jacket worn by valets of Oxford undergraduates in the seventeenth century. This etymology is based on the idea that the word for the jacket came to be applied to the servants themselves, some of whom were cheats and thieves.

A related disparaging term, but applied to a different nationality, is "welsh," to fail to fulfill an obligation, especially in the sense of not paying a lost bet. This cheating sense arose at racetracks in the mid-nineteenth century, when some bookmakers absconded with bets. Since some bookmakers were from Wales, long regarded by the English as the home of thieves, the term caught on more generally in this pejorative sense.

Other disparaging "welsh" terms include "welsh comb" (the thumb and four fingers); "welsh cricket" (a louse); "welsh carpet" (a painted floor); and "welsh rarebit," originally "welsh rabbit" (toasted bread and cheese, country humor dating back to Shakespeare's time). Even the word for a common food is an indirect slur on the Welsh. The invading Saxons contemptuously referred to the native Celts as "Wealhs," meaning "foreigners." The Saxons called the nut they found in the land of the Celts *wealhhnutu*. We call it a walnut.

Linguistic xenophobia is not limited to pejoratives about Flemings, Gypsies, and the Welsh. Here is a sampling of ways we have historically disparaged one another, usually with a good dose of irony: Chinese compliment (false compliment), Chinese fire drill (a chaotic condition), in Dutch (in trouble), Dutch treat (each person paying his or her own way), Dutch rose (a dent in wood when a carpenter misses a nail), French letter (condom, the French version being *une capote anglaise*), German comb (fingers), Greek (incomprehensible, as in "it's Greek to me!"), Indian giver (one who demands return of the gift), Irish triplets (three children in three years), Irish kiss (a slap in the face), Irish marathon (relay race), Italian perfume (garlic), Mexican breakfast (a glass of water and a cigarette), Mexican standoff (stalemate), and Scotch blessing (vehement scolding).

Even within our national borders we have such pejorative terms as a California prayer book (deck of cards), Michigan wad (roll of singles with a hundred-dollar bill on the outside), Georgia credit card (length of hose used to siphon gas out of another's tank), and Philadelphia lawyer (one expert in exploiting the law's technicalities to circumvent the law).

flavor | inflate

In Latin, *flare* meant "to blow," past participle *flatus*. Inflate, deflate, conflate, and soufflé all derive from this root, as does flavor. Vulgar Latin **flator*, derived from *flatus*, meant odor—literally, that which blows. This word evolved into Old French as *flaor*, and Middle English *flavour*, meaning aroma. Since the sense of taste relies very much on the aroma of food (our sense of smell is thousands of times more sensitive than our sense of taste), "flavor" came to mean the distinctive taste of a food. The first recorded use of "flavor" to mean "taste" is in Congreve's translation of Juvenal's *Eleventh Satire*, in 1697. Congreve described the taste benefit of eating fish when fresh, using words that could be used as a slogan today for a merchant of fresh fish: "If brought from far, it [Fish] very dear has cost, It has a Flavour then, which pleases most."

Latin *flare* evolved from Indo-European root *bhel-, meaning "to blow." Other words from this root are blow, bladder, blast, blather (to prattle), blaze, and blasé. The relatedness of "blow" and "blasé" is the notion that someone who is blasé lacks interest because of frequent exposure or indulgence, and therefore is tired of pleasures. It joins our lexicon via the past participle of French *blaser,* meaning initially "to be chronically hung over," and then more generally "to be exhausted with pleasure, satiated." The French apparently have some experience with this state of inebriation, as well as this state of pleasure.

forest | forfeit

The door to a house has literal as well as symbolic significance: the world outside that door is distinct from the world inside. Indo-European root *dhwer-, meaning "door" is the source of our word "door" and many words derived from Latin pertaining to phenomena occurring outside the door.

Derived from *dhwer-, Latin *foris* (being out of doors) is the source of both "forest" (our "great outdoors") and "foreign." If we are shut out of our homestead door, we are "foreclosed" by the legal process of a mortgage "foreclosure."

In ancient Rome, the enclosed space outside the front door of a home was called a *forum.* Over time, *forum* came to mean a marketplace, or a public place where people assembled for public business or judicial proceedings. "Forensic" describes debate or argument, or something relating to, used in, or appropriate for public discussion or for courts of law.

The same concept of "outside the door" appears in the more general sense of "out of bounds" in the word "forfeit." From Latin *foris* (outside) and *facere* (to make or do) evolved Old French *forfait*, past participle of *forfaire*, meaning "to act outside the law, commit a crime." If you act outside the law, or outside the rules, you are subject to surrendering something as a punishment. For example, John McEnroe once forfeited a tennis match in the Australian Open not for his out-of-bounds shots, but for his out-of-bounds tirade against the umpire.

One other word derived from *dhwer- takes us back to the door itself. Greek *thura* (door) and *thureos* (oblong shield) evolved to "thyroid," the gland located in front of and on either side of the trachea, the door to our windpipe.

franc | frankly

The Franks were a Germanic nation that conquered Gaul in the sixth century. They were named after their weapon of choice, the *franca*, a spear, just as the Saxons were named after their favorite weapon, the *seax*, a knife. The first written reference to this nation, as "Francna," was in the eighth century epic poem *Beowulf*. At the beginning of the fourteenth century, Chaucer was the first to describe the language of the Franks. In *Canterbury Tales*, Chaucer wrote of a "newe frenshe song."

The franc, the French unit of currency, is another word derived from the Franks. After King Jean II of France was captured in the battle of Poitiers, his captors freed him in 1360 so he could return to France and raise a ransom of three million gold crowns. In his attempt to accomplish this daunting task, he ordered a new gold coin struck, picturing himself on horseback on the coin's face, with the Latin legend: *Johannes Dei gracia Francorum rex*, meaning

"Jean, by the grace of God, King of the Franks." From this coin, and a similar one honoring his successor, Charles V, the word "franc" originated. It was originally known as a *franc d'or* (gold franc), and, embarrassingly, *franc des Anglais*—meaning that the king was "free of the English." (By the fourteenth century, "franc" acquired the meaning "free," because in Frankish Gaul only the dominant Franks possessed full freedom or the status of freemen.)

Other eponymous words derived ultimately from the Franks are the superior incense of the Franks, "frankincense"; the radioactive metallic element "francium" discovered by French chemist Marguerite Perey; the Anglicized French known as "Franglais," and the names France and Frank. For examples of Franglais, see chaise lounge/longitude.

As an extension of the "free" meaning of "franc," by the sixteenth century, "frank" came to mean "liberal and generous, open, sincere, candid," as in Shakespeare's early use in *Othello* (act I, scene 3): "Bearing with frank appearance their purposes toward Cyprus."

More specifically, "frank" came to mean "candid speech," as in Shakespeare's *Henry V* (act I, scene 2): "With franke and with uncurbed plainnesse." This usage gives us Rhett Butler's most memorable line in *Gone with the Wind*, when he drives an emotional spear into poor Scarlett O'Hara's heart: "Frankly, my dear, I don't give a damn."

The 1700s brought "frank" as the signature of a member of parliament entitled to send letters post-free, just as members of the U.S. legislature have "franking" privileges today.

Around 1800, an immigrant from Frankfurt, Germany, introduced in the United States the popular hot dog known as a "frankfurter." The German city Frankfurt, and people living there, *Frankfurters*, were so named because it was the "ford of the Franks," the place from which the Franks set out on their raids. "Frankfurter" was soon shortened to "frank," as in "Let's get some franks during the seventh-inning stretch!" Likewise, "hamburger" derives from Hamburg, Germany and the name for its residents, *Hamburgers*, because this type of steak was associated with that port city from which many immigrants came to the United States. Hamburg, in Old German, was Hammaburg, meaning forest city.

According to legend, the hamburger is a namesake for Hamburg, New York, where Germans first settled in the 1830s. Charles and Frank Menches, Ohio entrepreneurs, traveled a circuit of county fairs, selling sandwiches. In 1885, while at the Erie County Fair in Hamburg, New York, also known as the Hamburg Fair, they ran out of pork sausage, and substituted chopped meat. If this tale is not apocryphal, the hamburger is named for its birthplace, Hamburg, New York, and was so named as an inducement for German immigrants to settle in what was then the frontier. So even if this tale is true, the ultimate origin is Hamburg, Germany.

The first use of "Hamburg steak" for chopped meat, as recorded in the *Oxford English Dictionary*, was in a February 16, 1884, article in the *Boston Journal*, putting the claim of Hamburg, New York, in doubt. Other towns asserting their origin of the ground beef patty are New Haven, Connecticut (1895), Seymour, Wisconsin (1895), and Athens, Texas (1904), all postdating the *Boston Journal* article, and therefore all suspect. This chronology reinforces the conclusion that the source of this fast food and its name are the German immigrants from Hamburg who introduced it to America as part of their heritage. Before the fourteenth century, Russian Tartars introduced ground beef to the Germans, shredding low-quality beef to make it more edible and digestible. The Tartars also ate raw shredded meat (our steak tartare), and created a pungent sauce to go with it, presumably to make this carnivorous meal more palatable (our tartar sauce).

gazebo | placebo

A gazebo is a structure, such as a pavilion or summer house, built on a site affording an enjoyable view. A placebo is a substance having no pharmacological effect, given merely to satisfy a patient who supposes it to be medicine, or administered as a control in clinical tests. What these words have in common is expectation.

Gaze is probably of Scandinavian origin, from a word meaning "stare, gape." The "-ebo" of "gazebo" is a whimsical borrowing from the Latin first-person singular for "I will . . ." Literally, a gazebo is a place from which a person will gaze upon a scene, usually a garden. The earliest recorded use is from 1752 in a reference to "The Elevation of a Chinese Tower or Gazebo." (Because of this reference to a Chinese tower, some etymologists have suggested that "gazebo" derives from an unidentified Asian word, but this is mere speculation.)

Placebo is pure Latin, first-person future singular of the Latin verb *placere,* meaning "I will please." *Placere* and related Latin words are the source of our words please, plead, complacent, placid, and pleasant. The earliest recorded use of "placebo" was in 1785. Just as a person expects to gaze out on a lovely scene from a gazebo, a person expects to have a pleasing effect from a placebo.

gorge | gargantuan

The various meanings of "gorge" literally or figuratively pertain to the throat, from the Indo-European root *guer-, meaning "to swallow." As a verb, "gorge" means to stuff with food, and "disgorge" means either to vomit or to surrender ill-gotten gains, such as stolen goods or money. A mosquito is engorged with blood after biting its victim, and a convicted crook must disgorge what he stole.

As a noun, "gorge" refers to the stomach's contents after the food passes the throat, used figuratively in such statements as "the cruelty of war made my gorge rise." "Gorge" also refers to a deep ravine that forms a narrow passage.

"Gorge" entered the English lexicon from Old French *gorge,* meaning throat or bosom, via Vulgar Latin *gurga,* meaning "throat," which in turn derived from Latin *gurgulio,* meaning "gullet," and Latin *gurges,* meaning "throat, abyss, or whirlpool." Related Latin *regurgitare,* meaning "to engulf or flood," is the source of our word "regurgitate."

Less obviously related words from the same Indo-European root *guer- are bronchitis (from Greek *bronkhos,* meaning "throat or windpipe"), voracious and devour (both from Latin *vorare,* meaning "to swallow").

Gargantua, a well-known character in medieval French folklore, was a benevolent giant of voracious thirst and appetite. His name derived from Spanish and Portuguese *garganta,* meaning "gullet or throat." François Rabelais, the sixteenth-century French satirist, wrote a novel, *Gargantua,* whose central character's first words were "Drink, drink, drink!" and who once inadvertently swallowed five pilgrims while eating his salad.

The earliest recorded references to Gargantua in English appeared soon after the publication of Rabelais's novel of that name in 1534. One early reference, in 1593, alludes to the vivid salad incident: "Pore I . . . that am matched with such a Gargantuist, as can deuoure me quicke in a sallat." The first recorded use of "gargantuan" was in 1596, with reference to a "Gargantuan bag-pudding." Another early usage referred to a "Gargantuan bellyed-Doublet with huge sleeves."

Modern usages of "gargantuan" include descriptions of restaurant portions that could choke a python as coming in two sizes, "giant and gargantuan"; the purchase of foreign oil to satisfy "the gargantuan U.S. oil consumption"; a condemnation of the plethora of legal periodicals as churning out "a gargantuan soufflé of airy irrelevance"; and a description of Bill Clinton as "a man endlessly at war with a gargantuan appetite."

hack | hackneyed

Hackney, a borough in northeast London, was once a village in the outskirts of the capital where horses were raised before being taken to the city for sale or hire. This village may have been named for a word in use since the fourteenth century for an average quality horse used for hire, as in Chaucer's reference: "He . . . loved to have welle hors of prys . . . [but] he Hadde in his stable only hakeney." Most hired horses are past their prime, and thus there was a development in the meaning of the words "hackney" and its shortened form "hack," by the logic of association.

The original meaning, a worn-out horse, was extended to refer to a vehicle plying for hire, as in a "hackney" coach or carriage, or the driver of such a coach. By further extension, "hackney" and "hack" came to refer to any person whose services may be hired for any kind of work—including a prostitute or a lawyer. For example, in Henry Fielding's 1749 novel, *Tom Jones,* he describes the plight of one character: "Unluckily, a few miles before she entered that town, she met the hack attorney."

The meaning of "hackneyed" and "hack" further evolved to refer to a common drudge, especially a literary drudge who hires himself out to do any and every kind of literary work, a poor writer, or mere scribbler, as in a reference to "Grub Steet hacks" who had to write enough prose to pay their landlords. To this day, anything in indiscriminate and everyday use, trite, or commonplace, is "hackneyed," especially with reference to prose. We also have our tired and uninspired hack lawyers and preachers, and the political party hacks.

In any city today, you can travel by "hack"—a taxi, the modern equivalent of the hired horse from Hackney. In New York City, there is a Hack Poets Society of cabdrivers. Displaying a poetic as well as a cabbie's license, these hack poets combine all the elements of this eponymous etymology, epitomized in this hackneyed poem of a cabbie:

> Welcome to New York
> And for you I will not lag.
> I take care of your luggage
> for just five dollars a bag.
> I cannot turn the music down
> the button does not work.
> I try to fix it many times
> I think it is a quirk.

We now have computer hackers, but they probably derive their name from the sport of breaking into ("hacking" into) computer systems by outwitting them. This use of "hack"—etymologically unrealted to hack/hackney above—is onomatopoetic rather than eponymous, dating back to Old English *haccian,* and Indo-European root *keg-, meaning "hook or tooth," ultimately imitative of the sound of chopping. The computer "hacker" is the most recent addition to predecessor "hack" words from the same root, including the fourteenth-century tool ("hack," as in our "hacksaw"), the nineteenth-century term for a persistent cough ("hacking cough"), and the 1950s term for an inability to cope ("can't hack it"), all of which survive to this day.

hashish | assassin

At the time of the Crusades, members of a fanatical sect of Ismaili Muslims, part of the Shiite branch of Islam, pledged themselves to kill Christians and other enemies. Their fellow Syrians called them *hashishi* or *hashshash,* because they were reputed to have committed their murders under the influence of hashish. They murdered public figures in blind obedience to their leader, a condition brought on by their drug-induced state.

The name "hashish" for the dried plant creating this intoxication is from Arabic *hashsha,* meaning "it was dry." This word, which originally applied to plants generally, came to apply to a specific intoxicating plant, just as "grass" or "weed" became a term for the more specific marijuana plant.

As news of this murderous sect spread to Europe, Romance languages acquired words for its members, including Spanish *asesino* and French *assassin.* (In Arabic, the plural for hashish eaters is *hashshashin.*) English borrowed this term in the fourteenth century, probably from Middle French, when it first appeared as *hassassis.* The term "assassin" now applies to any murderer, of whatever sect, political persuasion, or state of intoxication.

hen | enchant

Hens don't sing, but roosters do. In fact, the rooster's crow is one of its distinguishing characteristics. In Old English, *hana* meant "rooster," reflected in the modern German word for crow, *Hahn*. Our word "rooster" is based on the word "roost," on which roosters perch. In the seventeenth century, this bird was known as a "cock" or "rooster cock," but the word "rooster" came to be strongly favored in the United States for euphemistic reasons. At least our linguistic prudery does not prohibit us from referring to the rooster's crow as "cock-a-doodle-doo," a reminder of the onomatopoetic source of the name of the bird formerly known as a cock.

As with other animal words such as squirrel, dodo, lynx, and reindeer, the name of the hen is based on its prominent feature. Even though hens only squawk, their name derives from Indo-European root *kan-, meaning "to sing." From this root we derive chant, cantata, canticle (a form of hymn), cantor (musical leader of a religious service), accent (the singsong of a person's speech), and cant (jargon, talk filled with platitudes, or whining speech). Someone who disavows a prior statement "recants." To recant, a person may need an "incentive," from Late Latin, *incentivum*, meaning "setting the tune, inciting," from *incinere*, meaning "to sound."

Other words ultimately derive from the same Indo-European root *kan-. "Charm" derives from Latin *carmen*, meaning "incantation," via Middle English *charme*, meaning "magic spell." In quantum physics, some subatomic particles known as quarks have "charm," a property that explains the absence of certain decay modes and accounts for the longevity of some particles.

"Enchant" derives from Latin *incantare*, meaning "to utter an incantation, cast a spell." The notion of casting a spell with song is most famously depicted in the *Odyssey* of Homer, when Odysseus is lashed to the mast of his ship to avert what would otherwise be his shipwrecked fate, beguiled by the enchanting song of the Sirens.

Our word "siren" for a seductive and willful woman (as in the expression "a screen siren" for such actresses as Hedy Lamarr, Jean

Harlow, Greta Garbo, and Claudette Colbert), and for the wailing police car device, both derive from the mythical Greek Sirens. They were sea nymphs, depicted as birds with women's heads, who lured sailors to destruction on the rocks by their enchanting song. The explanation for the shriek of an emergency vehicle being named for alluring song lies in the fact that the word *sirene*, before acquiring this specialized use, was the term for an acoustical device for producing musical tones, invented by a Frenchman in 1819.

hieroglyphics | clever

A person must be clever to decipher hieroglyphics, but it requires discernment to see the etymological link. Both derive from Indo-European root *gleubh-, meaning "to tear apart, split." Our words cleave (split), cloven (like the foot of cows), and cleft (as in Kirk Douglas's and Michael Douglas's cleft chins) all derive from this root. The "clove" of a garlic is easily split from the other cloves. "Cleave" in this sense is unrelated to "cleave" meaning to adhere, cling, stick fast, or be faithful. That "cleave" derives from Indo-European root *glei-bh-, from which we also derive "clay." "Cleave" and "cleave" are in a rare group of identically spelled homonymic antonyms. For other words that are their own antonyms, see broker/breakfast.

"Clever" derives from Middle English *cliver,* meaning nimble or skillful, the underlying notion being that a *cliver* person cuts to the heart of the matter. The first use of this word, around 1250, described the devil as "cliver on sinnes."

The link between *gleubh- and "hieroglyphics" is in Greek *gluphein* (to carve). When inscribing hieroglyphics on wet clay, the ancient Egyptians split the surface of the clay by making wedge-shaped impressions and pictorial symbols to represent meanings or sounds, or combinations of the two. Greek *hiero* (holy) provides the first two syllables of this word, which literally means "holy carvings."

hill | excellent

The unifying concept linking these words is prominence. Indo-European root *kel- meant "to be prominent." *Kel- evolved into Germanic *khulniz and our word "hill." Related cognates meaning "hill or mountain" in other Indo-European languages include French *colline*, Italian *colle*, Spanish and Romanian *colina*, Lithuanian *kalnas*, and Latvian *kalns*. *Kel- is also the source of such projecting words as "culminate" (figuratively, reach the summit), from Latin *culmen*, meaning "top or summit" and, via Latin *columna* (meaning "a projecting object or column") colonnade; column; and colonel, originally the leader of a column of troops. Via Greek *kolophon*, meaning summit or finishing touch, we derive colophon, which refers to a publisher's emblem, and to an inscription at the end of a book giving facts about its publication—the publisher's finishing touch.

The same Indo-European root evolved, via hypothetical Latin verb *cellere*, meaning "to rise, be high," combined with prefix *ex*, meaning "out," to Latin *excellere*, "to raise up, elevate, be eminent," source of our words excel, excellence, excellent, and the more obscure excelsior.

Excelsior is a packing material made of thin, curved wood shavings. Such shavings were originally used to stuff the mattresses of the Excelsior Mattress Company, based in New York State. In 1868, the company derived its name, and the name for its mattresses, from the state's seal, which has on its emblem the Latin word *excelsior*, meaning "ever higher."

Trademarks other than "excelsior" that have joined the lexicon as generic nouns include aspirin, Band-Aid, cellophane, cornflakes, Dictaphone, escalator, granola, Jell-O, kerosene, lanolin, linoleum, nylon, phonograph, shredded wheat, thermos, and zipper. British words that were once trademarks include aga (kitchen stove), hoover (vacuum cleaner), li-lo (air mattress), and biro (ballpoint pen). Trademarks and service marks that are in the process of becoming common nouns and therefore potentially unprotected include Coke, Formica, Frisbee, Jacuzzi, Laundromat, Mace, Scotch Tape, Styrofoam, Teflon, Vaseline, and Xerox.

"Excelsior" is noteworthy not only as a trademark that joined the lexicon, but also as one of hundreds of modern English words that are verbatim Latin. Some have the identical meaning for us as they had for the ancient Romans. Here are some examples: administrator, aloe, ambrosia, apex, atrium, basilica, cadaver, cannabis, census, chorus, consensus, defector, dictator, forceps, forum, honor, horror, ibis, inferior, instigator, lichen, major, minor, momentum, multiplex, narrator, odor, oh, onus, orchestra, pauper, phalanx, prior, progenitor, splendor, superior, umbrella, unanimous, vapor, victor, and viscera.

Other Latin words survived intact into English, although they had related but distinct meanings to the ancient Romans. Here are some examples, with the original Latin meanings: abacus (cupboard, gameboard, panel, tray), abdomen (belly), acumen (point, sting, cunning), alabaster (perfume box), area (open space, temple forecourt, park), arena (sand, beach), focus (hearth, fireplace, home, family), audio (I hear), bonus (good), calculator (arithmetic teacher, accountant), calculus (pebble), cancer (crab), cervix (neck), diva (goddess), femur (thigh), formula (shape, beauty, agreement), latex (fluid), liquor (liquid, sea), minister (servant), opera (work), placenta (pancake), pollen (fluid), rabies (madness), raptor (robber, abductor), rostrum (beak, snout, muzzle, bow of a ship), sublime (aloft), tango (I touch), video (I see), and vulva (wrapper, cover, female genitalia, and as a delicacy, a sow's womb).

hostile | hotel

The reciprocal duties of hospitality between guest and host provide the basis for Indo-European root *ghos-ti-, meaning "stranger, guest, and host." This duality inherent in *ghos-ti- produced doublets of antonyms: guest and host, hospitality and xenophobia.

*Ghos-ti- evolved into the Latin words *hostis*, meaning "stranger or enemy," hence "hostile" and *hospes,* meaning "host, guest, and stranger." These words evolved, via French, into our words hotel and hostel, as well as host (now meaning one who receives guests, but once meaning an army, an archaic meaning reflected in our use of "host" to mean a multitude), hostess, hospital, hospice, hospitality, and the more obscure hostler and ostler, both originally an inn employee who tended to horses, and now an employee who services large vehicles or engines, such as locomotives.

Hostage may derive from Old French *hoste,* meaning guest or host, and related Old French *ostage, hostage,* a person given as security or hostage, apparently originally a lodger held by a landlord as security. But hostage may instead derive from Indo-European *sed-, meaning "sit," from which we derive such words as sit, seat, set, saddle, soot, séance, settle, sedentary, sediment, sedate, and sedative. On this theory, hostage derives from Latin *obses, obsidis* (from Latin *ob,* against, and *sedere,* to sit) via Vulgar Latin *obsidaticum and Old French *hostage,* all referring to the condition of being held as security for fullfilling an undertaking. The modern sense of a person seized by a political group or by a criminal to obtain money, safe passage, or a political goal, was not recorded until the 1970s. If this theory is correct, "hostage" and "obsess" are doublets.

A distant relative in this family is Greek *xenos,* meaning stranger. The relationship to *ghos-ti is in its suffixed zero-grade form *ghsen-wo. (Say that aloud, and you will hear an approximation of the sound "xeno.") In 1898, when British chemist Sir William Ramsay isolated a strange unreactive gas (now used in lasers and strobe lights), he called it xenon. A person who suffers from xenophobia is unduly fearful or contemptuous of strangers or foreigners. "Xenotransplantation" is the donation of an organ from one species (such as a pig) to another (such as a human), possible only with genetic engineering.

Ghost, although a likely candidate as a stranger from the beyond, is not in this family, instead deriving from Indo-European *gheis-, meaning terrified or fearsome. *Gheis- is also the source of ghastly and aghast.

iceberg | burglar

Indo-European root *bhergh- meant "high," with derivatives refer-ring to hills and hill forts. An iceberg is, literally, a mountain of ice. From the same root, a belfry is a tower, a high place of safety (*frij means "safety, peace"). In Old English, a fortified town was referred to as a *burg,* from which we derive "burg," names for numerous cities that end "-burgh" (such as Pittsburgh), borough, and our words for people who live in these cities—the bourgeois, and bourgeoisie. The same root appears in a number of place names in German, such as the city of Hamburg, which itself gave us the name for chopped meat patties we put in buns, sometimes short-ened to "burgers," with variant form "cheeseburgers."

Latin *burgus* meant "fortress, castle." Someone who broke into such a fortress was, in Latin, a *burgator,* from *burgare,* to break open, commit burglary in. This word passed into Anglo-French as *burgesour,* and became our "burglar."

As a legal matter, the difference between a robber and a burglar is that a robber steals your wallet while you are walking down the street, whereas a burglar steals your valuables after breaking into your home.

incredulous | courage

Cultures throughout history have assigned special significance to the heart and associated it with thought and emotion. The ancient Egyptians, for example, considered the heart to be the most important organ, believing that it generated both thought and emotion. They embalmed bodies by removing all other organs, but left the heart intact, because they believed it played an important role in the afterlife.

Ancient Greeks thought the soul was associated with the heart. For example, in the *Iliad,* Homer describes what happened when Patroclus plunged a spear into Sarpedon's heart: "From the wide wound gushes out a stream of blood,/And the soul issued in the purple flood." Aristotle proposed the theory that emotion came from the heart, although Plato thought it came from the brain. In Hebrew, the word *lev,* meaning "heart," appears almost two hundred times in the Bible, always associated with emotional and spiritual behavior. In Christianity, the heart represents the place of divine love.

This sense of the heart as a seat of thought and emotion endures in our heart-related words. Indo-European root *kerd-, meaning "heart," is the source not only of words that relate to the organ itself, such as cardiac and cardiology. But it is also the source of our terms courage (acting with heart), encourage (give heartfelt enthusiasm), discourage (the opposite, a form of disheartening), cordial (close to the heart, and the alcoholic beverage we share with those close to our hearts), accord and concord (with hearts aligned), discord (the opposite), and record (a throwback to the time when writing was not commonplace, and people retained information "by heart"). These "cour-" and "cor-" words derive from Latin *cor, cordis,* meaning "heart."

From *kerd, Latin also derived *credere,* meaning "to believe." From *credere,* we have credo (literally, "I believe"), credit, credible, credence, credulous, and incredulous. From Old French *croire* (to believe) and *mis* (wrongly, as in "misconduct"), we have the word for a heretic and, more generally, a villain: a miscreant.

Of particular interest in this "heart" group is "misericord," a word with multiple and apparently disparate meanings: (1) relaxation of monastic rules, as a dispensation from fasting, and the room in a monastery used by monks who have been granted such a dispensation; (2) a bracket attached to the underside of a hinged seat in a church stall to lean against; and (3) a narrow dagger used in medieval times to deliver the death stroke to a seriously wounded knight.

"Misericord" derives from Latin *misericordia,* from *misericors* (merciful) and *misereri* (to feel pity), and is related to our words "miser" (from Latin *miser,* meaning "wretched") and "commiserate" (from Latin *commiseratus,* past participle of *commiserari,* meaning "to pity"). All the definitions of "misericord" have one thing in common: the notion of heartfelt mercy, whether applied to relieve the hunger of a fasting monk, the discomfort of the parishoner standing for long periods during religious services, or the agony of a knight who had suffered a grievous injury.

The heart has not always been the seat of love. In sixteenth-century England, the liver was the love center, as can be seen in many Shakespearean references. For example, in *As You Like It,* Rosalind offers to cure Oliver of love, describing how she had cured another lover:

> And thus I cured him; and this way will I take upon
> Me to wash your liver as clean as a sound sheep's
> Heart, that there shall not be one spot of love in't.

In other cultures, this sense of the liver as the love center endures. In Burmese, emotions, especially love, are attributed to the liver. For example, it is common to say in Rangoon and elsewhere in

Myanmar (formerly Burma) "I love you from my liver," to call someone "my liver," and for an unrequited lover to suffer from a "broken
liver." Likewise, in palindromically named Malayalam, a language of
south India, Malaysia, and Singapore, many emotions Western culture attributes to the heart are attributed to the liver.

Of course, the fact of the matter is that the heart is actually just
a pump for blood, and the liver just an organ to secrete bile. All
other attributes are the product of imagination and culture.

inoculate | binoculars

The ancient Romans developed a means to implant the bud of one
plant into another plant, a rudimentary form of grafting. Their
word for this process was *inoculatus,* past participle of *inoculare,* to
engraft, implant. *Inoculare* is a compound word from *in-,* with its
present day meaning, and *oculus,* a word meaning both "eye" and
"bud" (just as we refer to the bud on a potato as an eye). In the
fifteenth century, the word "inoculaten" joined the English lexicon,
with the same grafting reference.

In the eighteenth century, medical researchers discovered that
infecting someone with a small amount of virus (engrafting or
implanting the virus on the human subject) produced immunity
from disease. By analogy, they applied the word "inoculate" to that
process, even though the underlying "eye" sense is absent.

The same Latin root, *oculus,* evolved into our word "ocular,"
and, in the plural form, *oculi,* to our word "binoculars," the first element of which is *bini,* meaning "two at a time." For proper depth
perspective, you must use both eyes at the same time when using
this optical device. Binoculars were invented in the seventeenth century, and eventually became popular for use in French opera houses,
allowing patrons in the distant (and less expensive) seats to view the
performance as if they were right up front. The term "binoculars"
did not evolve until the 1870s.

Less obviously, *oculus* evolved to "inveigle," from Latin *aboculus,* "without sight," via Middle French *aveugler,* literally, "to blind the eyes." Someone who inveigles wins another over by coaxing, flattery, or artful talk, figuratively "blinding the eyes" of the person influenced by such manipulation. Another less obvious derivative of *oculus* may be "ferocious," via Latin *ferox,* meaning "wild-looking, or fierce."

Latin root *oculus* is derived from Indo-European *okw-, which evolved to our words eye, daisy (day's eye), ogle, eyelet, monocle, triceratops, autopsy, synopsis, optometry, ophthalmologist, and pinochle. Pinocchio's name likely derives from two Italian words meaning "pine-eyed." "Window" is also in this ocular family, for reasons you will discover in window/nirvana.

jacket | jack-o'-lantern

In the Bible, Isaac's second son was Ya'akobh (Jacob), the father of the twelve patriarchs (Gen. 23:24–34). His name was translated into Greek as Iakob, and into Latin as Jacobus. Via Old French "Jaques," in the late thirteenth century, "Jacke" and "Jakke" developed as surnames in Middle English. By the time Chaucer wrote *Canterbury Tales* around 1390, "Jacke" and "Jakke" had shifted to be first names, used so commonly as to refer to any common fellow.

"Jacket" derives from "Jacques," the nickname given to French peasants in the 1300s. These peasants wore a type of tunic, which in Old French was called a *jaque,* and in Middle French *jaquet.* This word entered English in the mid-fifteenth century as "jaket."

The precursor to our "jack-o'-lantern" originated in the seventeenth century, and applied to a man with a lantern or a night watchman, in the varied forms "Jack-with-the-Lantern," "Jack-a-Lanthorn," and "Jack of lanthorns." In the same century, "Jack with a Lanthorn" came to refer to a variety of luminous natural phenomena, also called *ignis fatuus* (Latin for "foolish fire"), "will-o'-the-wisp," and "friar's lantern." These are the phosphorescent lights hovering over swampy ground at night, caused by spontaneous combustion of gases formed by the rotting of organic matter. In Ireland, where there are vast bogs, these evanescent luminescences were thought to be the souls of the dead, wandering interminably. In his 1749 novel, *Tom Jones,* Henry Fielding refers to this phenomenon: "Partridge firmly believed that this light was a Jack with a lantern, or somewhat more mischievous." The term "jack-o'-lantern" was not used for this phenomeon in written form until the nineteenth century. The first recorded use of "jack-o'-lantern" for a carved pumpkin appears in Nathaniel Hawthorne's *Twice Told Tales,* published in 1837.

"Jack-o'-lantern" for the carved pumpkin derives from Irish folklore. Jack was a stingy, miserable old drunk who played tricks on family, friends, and even the devil. One day, he tricked the devil to climb a tree, then placed crosses around the trunk of the tree so the devil could not get down. Jack made the devil promise not to take his soul when he died. When Jack died, Saint Peter denied him entrance to heaven, and the devil kept his promise. So, Jack had nowhere to go, and had to wander about forever in the darkness between heaven and hell. Jack asked the devil how he could live with no light. The devil tossed him a live coal from the flames of hell to help him light his way. Jack placed it in a hollowed-out turnip, and since that day Jack has roamed the earth without a resting place.

Irish villagers once found their way through the dark of late autumn by the light of a lantern made from a turnip, beet, or other vegetable. On All Hallow's Eve (our Halloween), the Irish hollowed out turnips, rutabagas, gourds, potatoes, and beets, and placed a candle in them to ward off evil spirits and keep Jack away. These were the original jack-o'-lanterns. The Irish potato famine of the mid-nineteenth century prompted over 700,000 Irish to immigrate to America, bringing their traditions with them. Fat orange pumpkins were readily substituted for these smaller vegetables, and so was born the carved-out snaggle-toothed jack-o'-lantern common in Halloween festivities today.

Other Halloween traditions derive from Irish folklore. The Irish believed that, on Halloween, spirits of the dead leave the grave and seek out the warmth of their previous homes. Fearful villagers dressed up in costumes to scare them away, and left food and other treats at their doors to appease these spirits, so the spirits would not destroy their homes or crops. These traditions give fresh meaning to "trick or treat!"

The many descendants of "Jacke" and "Jakke" include Jack (any fellow), jack (money), jack (device to lift a heavy object), jack (a small flag, as in the Union Jack), jack (copulate), jack (playing card), jack up (lift, or inject a narcotic), jack someone around (tease, harass), jack one (hit a ball a great distance), Jack's house or Jack's place (privy, chamber pot, now the more formal "john"), jacks (the children's game), jack-in-the-box, jack-in-the-pulpit, jackknife, jackpot, jackdaw, jackeroo, jackfish, jackboot, jackhammer, lumberjack, and crackerjack (a remarkable person or thing, reinforced by the introduction in the late nineteenth century of the popcorn/peanut confection).

"Hijack," originally meaning to rob in transit, dates from the 1920s bootleg era. It is apparently a back formation of "hijacker," perhaps from "high(way)" and "jacker," one who holds up. Some etymologists have speculated that this word derives from the greeting with which robbers accosted their intended victims ("Hi, Jack!), or a robber's command ("High, Jack!). Others attribute this term to Chinese *hoi* (ocean) and *ts'ak* (robber), producing *hoi ts'ak* (pirate), although this etymology seems less likely. A terrorist who takes control of an airplane "skyjacks," and a criminal who wants the car and not merely its contents "carjacks." The multifaceted "-jack" has also been applied to a criminal who steals laptop computers: he "lapjacks."

"Jackanapes," referring to an impertinent, presumptuous young man, or impudent, mischievous child, had greater vogue centuries ago. Its meaning derived from the fact that in England, Jack was a common name for a tame male ape. William de la Pole, duke of Suffolk, had a coat of arms featuring the clog and chain of a trained monkey. In 1450, the duke was arrested and beheaded for alleged treason against Henry VI. He was derisively styled "the Ape-clogge" and later was dubbed "Jack Napes," or "Jacknapes." It is also possible that the "napes" of "jackanapes" is eponymous, referring to Naples, the source of many apes brought to England in the fifteenth century. "Jackanapes" went from being a personal insult to the unfortunate duke to being a general insult.

"Jackstraw," referring to a worthless person, was the name or nickname of Jack Straw, an itinerant priest and leader, who, with Wat Tyler, led the Peasant Revolt against Richard II in 1381. In the original march on London to petition the king to protest tax collection practices, Jack Straw and other protesters burned and wrecked so much property they incurred the wrath of many. Jack Straw must have been particularly hated, for his name quickly took on its present meaning, the earliest reference being in Chaucer's *Canterbury Tales*, written just a few years after that unsuccessful revolt.

The Scottish cousin of "Jack" is "Jock," whose many descendants include, jock (athlete), jock (athletic supporter), jock (computer programmer characterized by creating large brute-force programs), jockey (professional rider in horse races), jockey (to pilot, or drive, as in "jockey into position"), jockey (to trick, cheat, or maneuver skillfully), disc jockey, shock jock (outrageously insulting disc jockey), car jockey (valet), bench jockey (player who heckles the opposing team from the dugout), and chopper jockey (helicopter pilot).

For surnames that derive from "John" and "Jack," see patter/paternity.

journal | journey

Indo-European root *deiw- meant "to shine," "the (shining) sky," and the "sky god." The "shining," and therefore daytime or day sense, survives in words from this root via Latin *dies, diurnum,* meaning "day," such as the daily "diurnal" events, the "dial" that marks the day's hours, the "diet" that dictates how much you eat in a day, and the less obvious word for the evil day (Latin *dies malus*) which is "dismal."

From this same root, via Late Latin *diurnalis* (daily), we derive such words as "journey" (originally, a day's travel), the "journeyman" day laborer, the "sojourn" of a temporary stay, and "adjournment" of a meeting or court proceeding to another day. "Journal," in the fourteenth century, referred to a book containing the form of church service during the daily hours of worship, then evolved in the sixteenth century to refer to a daily personal record, and in the eighteenth century to refer to a daily newspaper. "Journalist" first appeared in the seventeenth century.

The *deiw root, meaning "sky god," survived in the name of Greek god "Zeus," the Roman god Jupiter (from Diu Pater, the "Sky Father"), and Germanic god Tiw, source of our word "Tuesday." They are all "deities." "Divine," as an adjective, means "godlike," and, as a verb, means "foretell, prophesy," presumably with the aid of the gods. If, when saying good-bye, you say *adieu,* or *adios,* you are conveying the idea "may God be with you," which is exactly what "good-bye" means, in shortened form.

jumbo | mumbo jumbo

There is no certainty about the origin of "jumbo," but there is agreement that it derives from an African language. It may derive from the word for "elephant" in various West African languages, for example Kongo *nzamba*, the Swahili word *jumbo*, meaning "chief," or abstracted from "Mumbo-Jumbo," a grotesque bogey or idol.

To understand how the African word "jumbo" became part of our lexicon, we must turn to that great American impresario and showman, P. T. Barnum. The famed London Zoo was once the home of one of the largest elephants ever in captivity, captured in 1869 by a hunting party in West Africa. Standing twelve feet tall, and weighing over six tons, Jumbo was a great favorite at the London Zoo, giving rides to thousands of children, and was beloved throughout England.

In 1882, to the great consternation of the British public, the London Zoological Society sold its largest asset to P. T. Barnum for $30,000. When word spread that Jumbo would soon leave London for the United States, popular enthusiasm took the form of Jumbo words. There were Jumbo cigars; Jumbo letterheads; Jumbo earrings, fans, hats, and ties; Jumbo underclothing and Jumbo overcoats; Jumbo boots; and even Jumbo perfumes (one can only wonder about the fragrance). The menus of London hotels listed Jumbo soups and hash, Jumbo fritters and stews, Jumbo salads and pies, and Jumbo ice cream (presumably, none of which included elephant as an ingredient). On the eve of Jumbo's departure for the United States, nearly five thousand curious and sorrowful Londoners and others made a last visit to Jumbo for a fond farewell.

Within six weeks of Jumbo's arrival in New York, Barnum, ever the incomparable showman, reaped $336,000 from his investment. He fueled public interest in Jumbo with hyperbolic fanfare, touting his celebrated behemoth as "the Only Mastodon on Earth," "a Colossus of International Character," "the Towering Monarch of his Mighty Race," and so on.

Jumbomania seized the United States as it had in England.

Enterprising merchants hawked Jumbo products, as had their London counterparts. In 1882, "Jumbo" became the trade name for a shade of gray. By 1897, "jumbo" came to mean "enormous," so widely understood that the Sears Roebuck catalog that year advertised a canned fruit specialty: "Peaches, Jumbo California, halves." To this day, you can buy the oxymoronic "jumbo shrimp."

"Jumbo" retained continued vitality through the decades. The 1950s brought "jumboburgers" and "jumboize," to enlarge a ship, especially a tanker, by inserting a new middle section between bow and stern. The 1960s produced the first "jumbo jets," sometimes merely referred to as "jumbos." There is a certain poetry in this imagery, especially considering the resemblance of a line of jumbo jets inching along on the tarmac, awaiting takeoff, to a line of elephants, trunk to tail, plodding along at the circus.

A more recent "jumbo" development was Sony Corporation's 1990 installation of a twenty-three-by-twenty-three-foot grid of 560 picture tubes high over Times Square, each about the size of a home television set, producing a jumbo-size extremely clear and bright picture. Sony's name for this humongous screen is "Jumbotron," combining the African *jumbo* with Greek suffix *-tron,* referring to devices or tools (as in "cyclotron"). Now, "Jumbotrons" are seen in sports stadiums and other venues around the world.

Even though Jumbo never wore pompoms, his name may derive from "mumbo jumbo," a Hobson-Jobson word from Mandingo *ma-ma-gyo-mbo,* meaning "magician who makes the troubled spirits of ancestors go away." (For more on Hobson-Jobson words, see chaise lounge/longitude.) In Mandingo, *mama* means "ancestor," and *dyumbo* means "pompom-wearer." Some Mandingo peoples in western Sudan believe that a high priest, the "Mama Dyumbo," had the power to protect his village from evil spirits.

According to English explorer Mungo Park, if a man of the Mandingo tribe of Senegal thought one of his wives talked too much, thereby causing dissension in his household, he or a friend wore the disguise of Mama Dyumbo, scared her with his masked appearance and tufted headdress, made hideous noises, seized the offending woman, and whipped her as punishment. In English "mumbo jumbo" came to mean confusing talk, gibberish, nonsense, or ritualistic activity intended to confuse, first recorded with this meaning in 1896.

Other words in our lexicon that may derive from African languages include banjo (Angolan Kimbunde language *mbanza*), boogie-woogie (Hausa *buga* and Mandingo *bugc,* meaning "beat drums"), chigger (Yoruba and Wolof *jiga*), goober (Bantu *nguba,* meaning "peanut"), hip and hepcat (West African *hipi,* meaning "to be aware," or Walof *hipicat,* meaning "one who has his eyes wide open"), jazz (possibly from African *jaiza,* meaning "the sound of distant drums," but of uncertain origin), jukebox (Wolof *dzug* or *dzog,* meaning "to misconduct oneself, to lead a disorderly life"), okra (Tshi *nkruman*), tote (Konga or Kikonga *tota,* meaning "to carry"), voodoo (Ewe and Fon *vodu,* meaning "spirit, demon, deity"), yam (Fulani *nyami,* meaning "to eat," and Twi *anyinam,* meaning "yam"), and zombie (Kikongo, Kimbundu, and Tshiluba *nzambi,* meaning "god," and Kikongo *zumbi,* meaning "fetish").

king | pregnant

Indo-European root *gen-, meaning "give birth," has given birth to numerous words, some more obviously related than others. In the obvious group are such words as generation, generic, genre, genus, genius, genealogy, genocide, primogenitor, heterogeneous, and miscegenation. In some words, such as cognate and pregnancy, the *gen- root loses its vowel. Pregnancy is, literally, the status prior to giving birth. Less obviously related are such words as engine, germ, germane, germinate, nascent, née, Nöel, renaissance, oxygen, pathogen, kin, kindred, king, and kindergarten.

"Kin" and "kindred" derive from *gen- via Old English *cyn(n),* meaning "race, family, kin"; and "king" derives from the same Indo-European root via Old English *cyning.* Likewise, "kind" (a group with common traits) derives from Old English *cynd* and "kind" (warm-hearted) derives from Old English *gecynde.* (For more on "kindergarten," see OK/kindergarten.) Words derived from *gen- beginning with an "n," such as naive, nation, native, nature, and innate, and those cited previously, evolved from Latin *gnasci, nasci* (present participle *nascens,* past participle *gnatus, natus*), meaning "born." Words in the *gen- family beginning ger- (such as germinate) evolved from Latin *germen,* meaning shoot, bud, embryo, and germ.

There are so many words from *gen- that a story could be written almost exclusively with its progeny. Here's one:

The **Genuineness** of the **General's Progeny**

Gentle and **benign King** Olf had a daughter, Trina. She had the **innate naïveté** of an **ingenue,** more so than **kindred** spirits of her **gender** in this **kingdom.** A **genteel** and **genial** but **disingenuous general** in the **nation's** army was no **gentleman.** Rather, this **puny gent** was a **degenerate genius** who **engineered malignant** plots that belied his **congenial nature.** His apparently **genuine,** seemingly **congenital kindness engendered** a **kind** of trust that disarmed the **king's kin.**

One day, Trina proclaimed: "I'm **pregnant** with the **general's progeny!**" The **general** denied it: "I'm not the **progenitor!** When the child was born, the **ingenious king** did a **gene** test to determine his next **generation's indigenous nature.** Proof: the **general** fathered the **neonate!**

lady | dough

As sexist as this etymology may be, the fact is that, historically, the woman's place *was* in the home—and more specifically, in the kitchen. Indo-European root *dheigh- meant "to form, build." In Old English, related word *hlaefdige* referred to the "bread kneader," from *hlaf* (bread) and *dige* (kneader). *Dige* derives from Old English *dag* (dough). Our pronunciation of "dough" loses the Old English hard *g* sound, while retaining the Old English hard *g* spelling, found in such words as "thought" and "knight." The *hlaefdige* was not just the bread kneader. She was also the head of the household.

Our word "lady" (from *hlaefdige,* shortened over centuries to *lavedi,* and then to *ladi*), has both an exalted and derogatory sense. Compare Lady (title of the wife of a baron, count, or other nobleman, and "Our Lady" for the Virgin Mary) with the use of "lady" in: "Hey, lady! Move your car, wouldya?" Jazz singer Billie Holiday was a stunning tall woman who carried herself proudly, earning her the nickname Lady Day. A regal jam session would include Lady Day, Duke Ellington, Nat King Cole, and the artist sometimes known as Prince (not to mention Queen Latifah).

The "ladybug" is so named because this beneficial insect, which feeds on destructive garden pests, was named in honor of the Virgin Mary. An alternate word for "ladybug" is "ladybird," found in the nickname of former First Lady Ladybird Johnson.

One Lady of special note is Lady Godiva, wife of Lord Leofric, earl of Mercia. Lady Godiva, who lived in the eleventh century, may have ridden naked on her horse through the streets of Coventry, or the story may be apocryphal. Either way, the account of her infamous ride did result in an expression for a voyeur who gets pleasure, especially sexual pleasure, from secretly watching others.

Here's the story: Lord Leofric levied a tax on the citizens of Coventry that they found oppressive. Lady Godiva asked her husband to repeal the tax. He promised to do so, presumably in jest, on the condition that she ride through town on horseback stark naked. She requested that everyone in town remain indoors with their shutters closed on the appointed day.

Confident that people would obey her request, Lady Godiva rode forth, as Tennyson put it in his poem "Godiva," "clothed on with chastity," having "shower'd the rippled ringlets to her knee." A tailor (or butcher, depending on which version of the story you believe) named Tom couldn't help himself, and observed her as she rode by. Tennyson describes this scoundrel and the consequences of his betrayal of trust:

> And one low churl, compact of thankless earth,
> The fatal byword of all years to come,
> Boring a little augur-hole in fear,
> Peep'd—but his eyes, before they had their will,
> Were shrivell'd into darkness in his head,
> And dropt before him. So the Powers, who wait
> On noble deeds, cancell'd a sense misused.

This story was originally told by an unknown writer in the twelfth century, about seventy-five years after Lady Godiva died.

"Peeping Tom," first recorded around 1796, now refers to any voyeur. So, whether or not Lady Godiva *did* ride through town naked (as depicted on the chocolate confection), and whether prurient Tom even existed, the term "Peeping Tom" has endured as a pejorative. W. H. Auden captured the essence of this expression: "Peeping Toms are never praised, like novelists or bird watchers, for their keenness of observation."

lettuce | galaxy

The common characteristic of lettuce and galaxy is a milky appearance. The Latin word for milk, *lac,* is the source of our words lactation (secretion of milk), lactose, lactase, and lactic acid (all substances found in milk), and café latte (espresso topped with steamed frothed milk). The Latin word for lettuce was *lactuca,* with reference to the milky white sap exuding from the stalk when cut.

The Greek word for galaxy was *galaxías,* originally an adjective, meaning "milky," from the noun *gála,* meaning "milk." We acquired "galaxy" via Late Latin *galaxias* and Old French *galaxie.* The term "Milky Way," which is the galaxy containing our solar system, is a translation of Latin *via lactea,* and is of about the same antiquity in

English as "galaxy." Ours is not the first generation to perceive of the myriad of stars as having a milky appearance.

All these words derive from Indo-European *g(a)lag-, *g(a)lakt-, meaning "milk." The word "milk" itself derives from Indo-European root *melg-, meaning "to rub off, to milk," via Old English *meolc, milc.* This root is also the source of "emulsion," from Latin *mulgere,* to milk.

lunatic | lynx

The unlikely common denominator for this doublet is Indo-European root *leuk- meaning "light, brightness." Words more obviously based on this root are light, lightning, luminuous, illuminate, luster, lucid, elucidate (figuratively, to make clear), pellucid (transparent or translucent), translucent, lumen (in physics, a unit of light), and the trademark for a transparent resin, Lucite. A luminary is an object, such as a star, that emits light, or a person who inspires others or who has achieved eminence in a specific field, such as a "cultural luminary."

"Lunar" refers to the moon, from Latin *luna* (moon), via Old French *lunaire*. In ancient Rome, someone who was epileptic was perceived as "moon-struck" (*lunaticus*), based on the astrological belief that recurrent attacks of insanity were caused by the varying phases of the moon. "Lunatic," recorded in English as early as 1290, now means insane, wildly or giddily foolish, or eccentric. Related word "loony" primarily means "extremely foolish or silly," with such spin-offs as loony bin for an insane asylum, and Looney Tunes for the Warner Brothers animated cartoons featuring such loony characters as Bugs Bunny, Elmer Fudd, and, most apt for this etymology, Daffy Duck.

How does "lynx" join this family of "bright" words? The lynx, like other cats, has a membranous region around the retina of its eyes called the *tapetum lucidum,* which reflects light back to the retina after it has passed through once, giving the cat two chances to capture an image, further enhancing night vision. This layer of iridescent cells reflects even the faintest light and explains why, when you photograph your cat with a flash, its eyes shine and why, if you shine a flashlight across the face of your cat in a dark room, you see the light flash back at you. The lynx is so named because of its shining eyes, a phenomenon noticed by people speaking a variety of languages over time: Latin (*lynx*), Greek (*lynx*), Old Prussian (*luysis*), Lithuanian (*lusis*), Armenian (*lusanunk*), German (*Luchs*), Dutch (*los*), and Old Saxon (*lohs*).

You could not put a lynx in a bag, but you could put a cat in a bag. Therein lies the source of the expression "let the cat out of the bag," which is inextricably linked to the expression "don't buy a pig in a poke." In England, a poke is a small sack and, historically, the word "pig" referred only to a very young swine. A peasant selling a piglet in a country market would place it in a poke. Because young swine were notoriously difficult to catch if released from the poke, unscrupulous sellers would substitute a cat for a pig. It was thus imprudent to buy "a pig in a poke." (The French have a similar expression, *acheter chat en poche*, which means "to purchase a cat in a bag.")

To avoid disappointment upon arriving home (after all, Brits don't eat cats), a canny buyer would require the seller to open the poke, sometimes revealing the seller's attempted ruse when a cat rather than a piglet jumped out of the bag. Now, whenever we divulge a secret, whether or not in a shady business deal, we "let the cat out of the bag."

Other words in this *leuk- family include luciferin, the name for the chemicals a firefly produces, enabling it to send visual Morse code signals. Luciferin produces bioluminescent light when oxidized under the catalytic effects of luciferase. "Luciferin" and "luciferase" derive from Latin *lucifer*, meaning "light-bringing."

Lucifer, another name for a friction match, for the planet Venus in its appearance as the morning star, and for Satan, likewise means "light-bringing," but this requires an explanation. Why should the prince of darkness, the archangel of hell, be named as someone who brings light?

We must turn to the Bible for an explanation. The king of Babylon was a mighty oppressor of the Hebrews. Like other sovereigns, he considered himself divine and referred to himself in celestial terms (compare Louis XIV's reference to himself as the Sun King). The word for the king of Babylon in Hebrew is *helel*, meaning "day star." Translated into Latin, *helel* became "Lucifer."

Upon his death, the king of Babylon met his just fate, as described in Isaiah 14:12 to 14:15:

> How you are fallen from heaven, O Day Star, son of Dawn!
> How you are cut down to the ground, you who laid the
>   nations low!
> You said in your heart, "I will ascend to heaven, above the
>   stars of God.
> I will set my throne on high. I will sit on the mount of
>   assembly in the far north.

I will ascend above the heights of the clouds. I will be like
the Most High.
Yet thou shalt be brought down to the sides of the Pit . . . .
You are brought down to Sheol, to the depths of the Pit.

maniac | automatic

The mind is capable of variant functions, giving rise to diverse
words from the Indo-European root *men-, meaning "to think,"
with derivatives referring to various states of mind and thought.
Obvious words that trace their lineage to *men- include mind,
mental, demented, comment, mention, reminiscent, and memento.
"Memento" suggests the reduplication of a memory, from Latin
reduplicated form *meminisse,* meaning "to remember." Your memory of an event is doubly enriched by your memento of it.

Other members of the *men- family are not as obvious. Mania,
maniac, and manic all derive from *men- via Greek *mania,* meaning
"madness." The related Greek-derived suffix -*mancy* means
"divination." If we engage in black magic and sorcery, or seek to
communicate with the sprits of the dead to predict the future, we
engage in "necromancy."

Also derived from *men- is the Greek suffix -*matos,* meaning
"willing." The Greek word *automatos,* for example, means "acting of
one's own will, self-acting." If something is self-willing, it is "automatic," whether with reference to an aircraft's automatic pilot, a
car's automatic transmission, or the automatic shrinking of our
pupils in a strong light. When "automatic" joined the lexicon (first
recorded in 1748), it was used with reference to what we now call the
autonomic nervous system, which regulates the self-induced invol-
untary actions of the intestines, heart, and glands. For example, you
don't have to think about digesting food or pumping blood—they
happen automatically. Now, the word "automatic" is typically used
with regard to machines, with the implicit suggestion that machines

act of their own free will. It is no surprise, then, that another related word is "automaton," meaning "robot."

In Greek, one whose mind sees into the future—a seer or prophet—was a *mántis*. In a subspecies of two disciplines, aptly described as either entymological etymology or etymological entymology, we turn to the Greeks, who made the connection between the upraised front legs of a certain predatory insect waiting for its prey and the hands of a prophet in prayer. They referred to this insect as a *mántis*, and we refer to it, redundantly, as a "praying mantis." Its technical name is, appropriately, *Mantis religiosa*.

The sense of using the mind for prayer and, more generally, for counsel, survives in words derived from Sanskrit *mántra-s*, meaning "prayer, hymn, counsel." In Hinduism, a "mantra" is a sacred verbal formula repeated in prayer or meditation. A "mandarin," originally with reference to a high public official in the Chinese Empire, now more generally refers to any high governmental official or bureaucrat. "Mandarin" derives from Sanskrit *mántra-s* via related Sanskrit word *mantrín* (adviser). The Hindi cognate is *mantri* (council or minister of state).

Names of Roman and Greek mythical characters likewise derive from *men-. Minerva was the Roman goddess of wisdom, invention, the arts, and martial prowess. Mentor was Odysseus's trusted friend and counselor, whom Odysseus left in charge of his household while Odysseus went off to fight the Trojan War (*The Iliad*), and while having fantastic adventures on his way back home (*The Odyssey*). Mentor (Athena in disguise) guided Odysseus's son, Telemachus, in his search for his father. At the end of the seventeenth century, the French author Fénelon included Mentor as a character in his romance *Télémaque*. Within fifty years, the word "mentor," in both French and English, had come to mean "a wise counselor or teacher." This is fitting, since Mentor's name probably meant, literally, "adviser" in Greek.

"Mentor" is a suitable member of the *men- family. It belongs— worth not just comment, but the highest accolades—because a true mentor can transmit knowledge from one generation to the next, for an enduring legacy. As Samuel Johnson put it: "He that teaches us anything which we knew not before is undoubtedly to be reverenced as a master." Indeed, Aristotle placed teachers above parents: "Teachers, who educate children, deserve more honor than parents, who merely gave them birth; for the latter provided mere life, while the former ensure a good life."

For other doublets based on *men-, see admonish/money and amnesty/mnemonic.

menu | minute

In Latin, *minutus* means "small." The Latin expression *minuta scriptura* denoted the small writing of a rough draft, which we describe as our "minutes" of a meeting. The French descendant of *minutus* is *menu*. The extended use of "menu" to mean "detailed" led to its use as a noun meaning "list," and the French expression *menu de repas*—menu list—and eventually our "menu."

In medieval Latin, *pars minuta prima*, literally "first small part," applied to a sixtieth part of a whole, first of a circle, then of an hour. Thus, a "minute" is a sixtieth of an hour. A further division—or second cut, in Latin *secunda minuta,* is a sixtieth of a sixtieth—the split "second" shown by the second hand on a watch.

Other words derived from the same Latin source include minute (tiny), mince, mincemeat, minimum, minor, minority, miniskirt, minus, minuscule, minutia, diminish, miniature, and the less obvious minister (originally, an inferior or servant, from Latin *minister*), ministry, minestrone (from Latin, *ministrare,* to serve food, via Old Italian, *minestrare*), minstrel (originally, a servant or entertainer), minuet (originally, a slow dance of small steps), and possibly minnow (the tiny freshwater fish).

The word "minimum" gives rise to a small but intriguing point. On the printed page, even without dotting the *i*s, "minimum" can be read. But in script, without dotting the *i*s, "minimum" could be read as "murumum," "nunmum," or other gibberish. Try writing "minimum" in script without dotting your *i*s and see for yourself. To bring the point home, write "skiing" without dots and you get "skung."

Why do we dot our *i*s, and *j*s, for that matter? Unlike other languages with diacritic marks, such as the cedilla, tilde, circumflex, macron, grave, and umlaut, plus more than ten others in Hebrew alone, English has no free-floating marks above or below letters, except for the requirement that we dot our *i*s and *j*s. We dot these letters so we don't lose sight of skinny *i* and, by extension, *j*. Capital *I*, sturdy as a steel I beam, needs no dot, nor did its predecessor, Greek *iota*, derived from Semitic *yod*, a pictogram for the arm.

Scribes in the eleventh century saw fit to signal the lowly *i* with this adornment in manuscripting such Latin words as *ingenii*, to avoid confusion with *ingenu*. Likewise, scribes dotted their *i*s when juxtaposed with *m, n,* and *u,* as when writing "minimum." By the fifteenth century, the dot developed into a long flourish and was used with *i* in all positions. In Roman type, the flourish was once again diminished to a dot. This dot, unlike other diacritic marks, did not convey information about pronunciation of a letter, but instead was a marker of its very existence. It was the buoy that scribes used to prevent hapless *i* from drowning in a sea of cursive swirls.

The same reasoning that led to dotting *i*s contributed to the formation of *j*. When *i* was the final letter, it was elongated to make it more distinctive, extending below the line, just as dotting it extended the letter above the line without making it into an *l*. This use of *j* was particularly evident where a word ended in two *i*s, as transforming *ingenii* to *ingenij*. Lowercase Roman numerals were written ij, iij, viij, and so forth. A similar use of *j* is found in Dutch, Swedish, and Icelandic, as in the first name of Swedish tennis player Bjorn Borg and the name of the Icelandic pop star Bjork. (For a discussion of Bjork's last name, see patter/paternity.)

J was very little used in English until the seventeenth century, because *y* had been substituted for the final *i*, a scribal canon having developed that no word could end with an *i*. This explains such formations as city-cities, holy-holier, carry-carries, weary-wearisome, as well as the evolution of calendar words from Maii to May, Iuli to July, and Fridaei to Friday.

Other letters of our alphabet besides *i* and *j* ultimately derive from Semitic letters based on pictograms. For example, the letter *m* is derived from *mem* in the proto-Sinaitic pictographic alphabet, which evolved from Egyptian hieroglyphics. This alphabet was used by the Hebrew slaves in Egypt during their enslavement and exodus from Egypt. *Mem,* a pictogram representing a stream of water or waves in the sea, was a horizontal zigzag pattern depicting six waves. *Mem* began with the same sound as our letter *m* and was the thirteenth letter of the alphabet, as is *m.* In Phoenician and Ancient Hebrew, *mem* was switched to the vertical position. According to rules that remain obscure, *mem* reassumed a horizontal position, and the number of its zigzags decreased to evolve to the modern Hebrew letter, which, like our *m,* retains only two wave patterns at the top. (In modern Hebrew, the word for water, which begins with *mem,* is *mayim.*) Our *m* evolved from Phoenician via Greek *mu,* which passed into Latin and thence to western European alphabets.

Similarly, our letter *o* was once a pictogram for an eye, *p* a pictogram for a mouth, and *b* a pictogram for a house. The similarity between the pictograms and the letters can be seen in the parallel Hebrew letters *ayin* (ע), *peh* (פ—an ancient precursor to the ubiquitous smiley face?), and *beth* (ב—complete with floor, wall, roof, and entrance). Hebrew letter *gimel* (ג), originally a pictogram for a camel, is the source of our letter *c. Gimmel* is the first letter of Hebrew *gamal,* from which we derive our word "camel."

mug | mugging

The word "mug" is likely of Scandinavian origin. In Swedish, *mugg* means "mug or jug," and in Norwegian *mugge* means "pitcher or heavy drinking cup." The slang sense for a person's face dates back to the beginning of the eighteenth century, when drinking mugs were

often made in the shape of grotesque human faces. By extension, in the nineteenth century the word "mug" came to refer to a photo of a person's face and, more specifically to a police "mug shot."

The verb "mug" to mean "attack" originated as a boxing term meaning "to strike in the face." In the mid-nineteenth century, this verb was extended to mean "to hit, beat up, attack with the intent to rob." The slang sense of exaggerating one's facial expressions (as in "to mug for the camera") is first recorded in Dickens's *Little Dorrit*, published in 1855.

In British slang, "to be had for a mug" means "to be taken for a dope," "a mug's game" is a profitless endeavor, and to "mug up" is to bone up, as for an examination. In Australian slang, a "mug" is a fool or incompetent person, and a person described as "two bob mug lair" is prone to showing off.

muscle | mouse

That the rippling flesh of a bodybuilder resembles the scurrying of a little mouse is not a modern observation. In Latin, *mus* is "mouse," and *musculus* is "little mouse." The Romans used the same

word, *musculus,* to mean "muscle," just as the Greeks used the word *mys* in both senses. From *mys* we derive "myo-" words, such as "myocardium," the muscular tissue of the heart. The Romans also saw the resemblance between a little mouse and the shellfish we know of as the "mussel." They used the same word, *musculus,* for it as well.

With a little imagination, the deer gland that secretes a strong odor used in perfumes looks like a little mouse. Observing this similarity, the Romans called the substance from that gland *muscus,* and we call it "musk" (although this etymology is not certain). The grape that smells like musk is "muscat," which, when fermented, produces "muscatel" wine.

Other "musk"-related words are the odoriferous muskrat, musk ox, musk rose, and muskmelon, and the deceptively named Muscovy duck. This duck, a native of South America, derives its name from an alteration of "musk duck," based on its musky odor, and not from the principality "Muscovy" founded in the thirteenth century, centered in ancient Moscow, and an archaic name for Moscow and more generally for Russia.

noon | nine

In ancient Rome, the hours of the day were counted from sunrise to sunset. Sunrise averages about 6:00 A.M., so the ninth hour, Latin *nona hora*, was 3:00 P.M. In Old English, the canonical hour of *nones*, also 3:00 P.M., was a time for church prayers. In Middle English, *nones* became *non*. Its meaning shifted from the ninth to the sixth hour when the time for church prayers was set three hours earlier in the day (that is, at noon).

By the twelfth century, "noon" meant the midday meal, and by the early thirteenth century, it meant midday. And so the "noon" hour derives from nine rather than twelve, based on historical rather than arithmetic logic, just as November, based on the Latin word for nine (*novem*) is not our ninth month, even though it was when the Romans began their year in March.

For a related development, consider "siesta," the daytime rest or nap. The sixth hour in ancient Rome was *sexta hora*, which is our noon. Spanish for "six" is *seis*. The "siesta" is so called because it was customarily taken during the midday.

One last example of a word out of time with its root word is "matinee" for the afternoon musical or dramatic performance. It derives from French *matin*, meaning "morning."

nostril | thrill

There is poetry in the link between these apparently unrelated words. The first syllable of "nostril" derives from Indo-European *nas-, meaning "nose," source of nose, nasal, nuzzle, nozzle, pince-nez glasses (eyeglasses with no temples that stay on by pinching the nose), and the name for the nasturtium plant. The nasturtium, a kind of cress, is so named because its acrid smell figuratively causes the nose (Latin *nasus*) to twist (Latin *torquere*).

The second syllable of "nostril" provides the unifying concept. Indo-European *terə- meant "to cross over, overcome" and is the source of the words through, thorough, and thrill. In Old English, *thryl* meant "hole," with verb form *thrylian*, "to pierce." By the four-teenth century, these words took on a variety of meanings, including "to break through enemy lines."

In the sixteenth century, the notion of making a hole led to the metaphorical notion of "piercing with emotion," first recorded in Shakespeare's *Romeo and Juliet* (1592). Juliet, when planning to drink a potion the morning of her wedding to Paris, to give her the appearance of death, shudders: "I have a faint cold fear thrills through my veins/ That almost freezes up the heat of life." (act 4, scene 3). By the nineteenth century, the meaning of "thrill" nar-rowed to "fill with pleasure," although the earlier meaning survives in the "thriller."

OK | kindergarten

H. L. Mencken described "OK," a word of unsurpassed versatility understood everywhere around the globe, as "the most shining and successful Americanism ever invented." Variants include the jocular "okeydoke," astronauts' "A-OK," the clipped "K," and the hand ges-ture, forming an *O* with the thumb and forefinger, while raising the other three fingers.

Many theories have been suggested for this *sine qua non* of com-mon parlance, including Choctaw Indian *okeh*, espoused by President Woodrow Wilson; the apocryphal story of Andrew Jackson approving documents as "orl korrect" ("all correct"); West African *wakey*; and American sailors' reference to the Haitian port of Aux Cayes (pro-nounced oh-kay), renowned for superior rum, as "OK" and, by exten-sion, their reference to anything worth approval as "OK."

The most commonly accepted etymology, however, derives from the 1830s, a time of an abbreviation fad among the young and fashionable set in U.S. cities. One example of this fad is reported in an 1839 newspaper account of an au courant young lady remarking to her escort "O.K.K.B.W.P.," which her suitor was to understand to mean "one kind kiss before we part." A modern variant is college slang "C.S.P." for the "casual sex partner" one sleeps with but to whom one is not committed. Dating customs have certainly evolved over the last century.

At the height of the initials craze, it became popular to use deliberate misspellings, and so "A.R." (all right) became "O.W." and "N.G." (no go) became "K.G." "K.K.K." meant "commit no nuisance," and "O.K." meant "all correct." The earliest recorded references to "O.K." appeared in 1839 articles in New England newspapers. Here is an example from the *Boston Evening Transcript:* "Our Bank Directors have not thought it worth their while to call a meeting, even for consultation, on the subject. It is O.K. (all correct) in this quarter."

"O.K." would likely have passed into oblivion with the other misspellings if not for the presidential election of 1840. (Only the periods in "O.K." have passed into oblivion, as superfluous.) Martin Van Buren was up for reelection, facing a tough fight againt General William Henry Harrison, the legendary hero who fought against the Indians at Tippecanoe, and his vicepresidential running mate, Virginian John Tyler. Van Buren and his handlers (precursors to our modern spin doctors) had to come up with a slogan as catchy as "Tippecanoe and Tyler Too."

To make matters worse, Harrison's followers dubbed Van Buren "King Martin the First," identifying him with the aristocracy. The Democrats' slogan had to counter this negative campaign tactic. They succeeded in doing so in the spring of 1840.

On March 27, 1840, radical Democrats in New York City, called Locofocos, broke into a Whig meeting, shouting a slogan that was based on their new organization, the O.K. Club, formed to campaign for Van Buren's reelection. Their slogan, dutifully reported in the press, was "Down with the Whigs, boys, O.K.!" The Whigs made political hay guessing the meaning of the cryptic "O.K.," which the Locofocos kept a secret, suggesting "Out of Kash," "Out of Kredit," "Out of Karacter," "Out of Klothes," and "Orful Kalamity." The anti-Locofos *New York Times* reversed the initials, running an April 6, 1840, headline: "K.O., KICKED OUT."

By late May 1840, "O.K." had become such a popular expression in New York that the Locofocos decided to reveal its meaning. On May 27, 1840, the *New Era,* a Locofocos paper, announced: "The very frightful letters O.K. [are] significant of the birth-place of Martin Van Buren, Old Kinderhook . . . the rallying word of the Democracy." By identifying Van Buren with his humble beginnings in the small village of Old Kinderhook, New York, the Democrats hoped to dispel the image of Van Buren as an aristocrat.

Van Buren lost the election, in part because even voters who remembered the intended meaning of "O.K." didn't forget the Panic of 1837. The Whigs made the most of Van Buren's loss, turning "O.K" back on him with its new meaning: "Off to Kinderhook." Even though he lost the election, he won a place in history. Today, those in the know ("I.T.N.?") understand that we refer to Van Buren's birthplace every time we say "OK."

Van Buren's hometown derived its name from the experience of the first Dutch settlers in the area. In the 1670s, Dutch residents of New Amsterdam (now New York City) decided to leave their crowded city and moved up the Hudson River. They found their new homestead about a hundred miles upriver, in an area inhabited by the peaceful Mohican Indians.

These Dutch settlers called this bucolic setting, much preferable for raising children than New Amsterdam, Kinderhook. *Kinder* is the genitive plural of German *Kind,* meaning "child," which ultimately derives from Indo-European root *gen-. "Hook" refers to a river bay. In Dutch, *hoek* means "corner."

Garten in German means "garden." Thus, a kindergarten is literally a children's garden. The German word *Kinder-Gartens* was coined in 1840 by educator Friedrich Fröbel, who opened the first such school in 1837, for developing the intelligence of children through such activities as doing exercises with toys, playing games, singing, and learning object lessons. The first English kindergarten was established in 1850, and the first recorded use of "kindergarten" in English appears in 1852.

Thanks to the symbols that grace every computer keyboard, we are able to venture well beyond the limitations imposed on Martin van Buren's supporters. Indeed, if you type into a computer with certain software :) and : (out pop ☺ and ☹.

The proto-smiley face was created in 1963 by Harvey R. Ball, of Worcester, Massachusetts (not Forrest Gump). A client of Mr. Ball's public relations agency merged with another company, and employees were not happy about the merger. He was asked to devise a promotional device to mollify the workers, and thus the smiley face was born. It took the country by storm once it caught on—in 1971 alone, more than fifty million smiley face buttons were sold, and in 1999 the U.S. Postal Service issued a smiley face stamp. It remains to be seen whether the U.S. Postal Service, which sponsors Lance Armstrong's victorious Tour de France cycling team, will put a smiley face on his jersey.

Just as Indo-European roots evolved in Darwinian fashion to a variety of words with disparate but related meanings, so the proto-smiley face evolved to express a variety of facial expressions beyond happiness and unhappiness, including (all to be read sideways):

indifference	: I
flirtatiousness	;)
crying	;- (
shock	:-0
sarcasm	:-]

More exotic species of smileys include:

a drunk	:*)
a punk	-:- (
a member of the clergy	+:-)
an angel	0:-)

Here's a smiley story: :-)   8-)   8- {) .   Translation: A smiley, to disguise himself, gets glasses and adds a fake mustache. As minitelephones develop minikeyboards with tiny screens, the use of abbreviations and symbols for words has proliferated, and a family of smileys will likely proliferate with them.

oxygen | vinegar

In 1786, when French chemists Guyton de Morveau and Antoine Lavoisier isolated a chemical element that they believed to be essential in the formation of acids, they turned to the Greek language to name it. Combining *oxýs* (acid, sharp) with *génos* (birth), they called the element *oxygène*. The second syllable of oxygen is a common suffix in chemistry and usually refers to something that produces or causes, found in such words as hydrogen, nitrogen, allergen, antigen, collagen, estrogen, pathogen, and carcinogen. For more on "-gen," see king/pregnant.

The same "sharp" sense of the first syllable appears in other "oxy" words, such as "paroxysm," a sudden outburst of emotion, attack of disease, spasm, or convulsion; "oxyuriasis," an infestation of pinworms; and "oxymoron," a pointedly foolish, paradoxical word or phrase bringing opposites together.

"Oxymoron" derives from Greek *oxýmōron,* meaning "sharp and dull, as in dull-witted." A prime example of an oxymoron is "sophomore," combining Greek *sophós* (wise) and *mōrós* (foolish) to describe the level of knowledge of a student in the second year of high school or college. Here are a few other examples: bittersweet, jumbo shrimp, old news, drag race, near miss, industrial park, living legend, open secret, deafening silence, hopeless optimist, light heavyweight, home office (and its corollary, working vacation), cold sweat, civil war, accidentally on purpose, good grief, baby grand, resident alien, terribly cute, pretty ugly, friendly fire, fresh frozen, same difference, Department of Interior (responsible for everything outside), inside out, definite maybe, and plastic silverware. Add to these some especially ironic oxymorons: military intelligence, legal brief, the statement "Thank God I'm an athiest," and the only words found on an otherwise blank space in some contracts (to assure that no devious party to a contract inserts language never agreed upon): "THIS SPACE LEFT INTENTIONALLY BLANK."

From an etymological perspective, two oxymorons of particular interest are freezer burn and guest host. Both "freeze" and "burn" derive from Indo-European root *preus- (to freeze, burn), and both "guest" and "host" derive from Indo-European root *ghos-ti. For more on guest and host, see hostile/hotel.

Greek *oxys* derives from Indo-European *ak-, meaning sharp or pointed. From *ak- evolved the Latin words *acus*, meaning "needle," *acutus*, meaning "sharp," *acidus*, meaning "sour," and *acer, acerbus*, meaning "bitter, sharp, or tart."

"Vinegar" derives from Latin *vinum acer* (sour wine), via Old French *vyn egre*. "Vinaigrette," originally a small French carriage resembling a vinegar-seller's cart, is an oil and vinegar dressing for salads. The ancient Romans served vinegar in a cup they called an *acetabulum*. Appropriately, anatomists apply this word to the cup-shaped cavity at the base of the hipbone into which the ball-shaped head of the leg bone fits.

These Latin roots produced sharp and sour literal and figurative words in our lexicon, including acuity (acuteness of perception, keenness), acumen (keenness of judgment), acute (keenly perceptive, as well as the sharply pointed angle of less than ninety degrees), acupuncture (a technique to relieve pain using thin needles), aglet (the needlelike end of a shoelace to make it easier to lace it up), acid (referring both to the sour chemical and the biting wit), acrid (sharp smelling), acrimony (bitterness), eager (showing keen interest, intense desire), acerbic (sour or bitter in taste, character, or tone), exacerbate (make worse, embitter, aggravate), and eglantine (a prickly-stemmed flower, also known as sweetbrier).

Related Greek words are *ake* (point) and *akón* (whetstone). A whetstone is a hard black stone, such as jasper or basalt, which the Greeks used to test the quality of gold or silver by comparing the streak left on the stone by one of those precious metals with that of a standard alloy. Greek *parakónē*, combining *akónē* with *para* (on the side), meant sharpening stone. This word evolved into Italian *paragone* and our word "paragon," a model of excellence or perfection by which others are compared. For more on "paragon," see parallel/paramecium.

Yet another Greek derivative from Indo-European *ak- is *ákros*, meaning topmost, tip, point, or high point. Greek *akróbatos* (going on tiptoe, climbing up high) is the source of our word for the high-wire trapeze-swinging acrobat. An "acropolis" is a citadel on a cliff around which ancient Greek cities grew, the most famous of which is the Acropolis in Athens, site of the Parthenon. When in 1825 industrialist General Simon Perkins founded a settlement at the highest spot on the canal route in Ohio, he called it Akron, based on this Greek root. Akron is located, appropriately, in Summit County, which boasts the highest altitude in Ohio.

An "acronym" (literally a "high-point name") is a word formed from the initial letters of words. For example, NATO is the acronym for North Atlantic Treaty Organization. Some words are not obviously acronyms. Examples include scuba (self-contained underwater breathing apparatus), radar (radio detecting and ranging), sonar (sound navigation and ranging), loran (long-range navigation), and laser (light amplification by stimulated emission of radiation). Other words are obviously acronymic, compact expressions of what would otherwise be tongue-twisting sesquipedalian terms difficult to remember or pronounce, such as LSD (lysergic acid diethylamide), CFCs (chlorofluorocarbons), HIV (human immunodeficiency virus), AIDS (acquired immune deficiency syndrome), CAT scans (computerized axial tomography scanning), and DNA (deoxyribonucleic acid).

Acronyms abound. We bank at ATMs, watch movies on our VCRs (when not watching sitcoms) both in the A.M. and P.M., listen to and invest in CDs, and use CD ROMs on our PCs. Observers of society have classified us into groups, such as yuppies (young urban professionals), yaps (young aspiring professionals), yumpies (young upwardly mobile professionals), guppies (gay urban professionals), puppies (parents of urban professionals), dinks (double income, no kids), oinks (one income, no kids), nilkies (no income, lots of kids), tinkies (two incomes, nannie and kids), glams (graying leisured affluent middle-aged), woopies (well-off older people), and zuppies (zestful upscale people in their prime). People who object to building such things as incinerators, prisons, or shelters for the homeless in their neighborhoods are nimbys (not in my backyard).

Acronymic computer terms beyond CD ROMs and PCs proliferate, including, just by way of example, PANS (pretty amazing new stuff), and PONA (persons of no account, i.e., not online). There are so many such terms, in fact, that computer nerds have acronyms for acronyms: the TLA (three-letter acronym), ETLA (extended three-letter acronym), SFLA (stupid four-letter acronym), and the British YABA (yet another bloody acronym). Here are a few more whimsical computer acronyms: a computer problem that is profoundly uninteresting and unlikely to benefit anyone else is a WOMBAT (waste of money, brains, and time); a badly designed computer program is BAD (broken as designed); and a computer system in which what appears on the screen exactly mirrors the eventual output is WYSIWYG (what you see is what you get).

The military industrial complex spawned so many acronyms they fill a book. More than thirty years ago, Raytheon Company compiled a book of such acronyms, titling it with the acronym *ABRACADABRA* (Abbreviations and Related Acronyms Associated with Defense, Astronautics, Business, and Radio-electronics), proving that even defense contractors have a sense of humor.

Indo-European root *ak- also produced the Greek word *akmé* (point), source of both acme (the highest point, perfection), acne, and Latin *ocris* (jagged mountain), from which we derive "mediocre," for a person or thing figuratively only halfway up the mountain. Thus, metaphorically, those who make it to the top are the acme, but those who ascend only midway are merely mediocre. Acme is a popular name for business ventures. In New York City alone there are nearly fifty companies so named, including the apparently redundant Acme Tip Printing Co. and Acme Top Company. Unsurprisingly, there are no companies in New York City named Mediocre Company, or any variation of that name.

One final point: Germanic descendents of Indo-European *ak- yield our words edge, egg (as in egg on), and ear (as in ear of corn). Each ear of corn growing on the stalk resembles a spike.

palindrome | dromedary

In Greek, *drómos* meant "a running, course, race course," and *dromás* referred to a camel bred for running. This evolved into Latin as *dromas*, genitive *dromadis*, and into Late Latin *dromedarius* for a camel. *Dromedarius* evolved into Old French as *dromadaire*, and our "dromedary" camel. The same *drómos* root appears in an obscure but useful word to describe a specific kind of fear: someone who fears subways is a "bathysiderodromophobe." This highfalutin word for this deep-seated fear is a compound of "bathy" (deep), "sidero" (iron), "dromo" (course or track), and "phobe" (fear).

"Syndrome" derives from Greek *sýndromos,* meaning "a running together." This is apt, since a syndrome is a group of symptoms that collectively indicate or characterize a disease or psychological disorder. A hippodrome is the arena for equestrian performances, literally, a racecourse for horses.

The same "running" sense survives in "palindrome," a word, verse, sentence, or numeral that reads the same backward and forward. The last syllable derives from the same Greek root, *drómos.* *Pálin-* in Greek meant "again," and *palíndromos* in Greek meant "recurrence"—literally, "a running back again." A palindrome "runs back" on itself, the same as when it "runs forward." Palindromes may have been invented by third-century B.C. Greek poet Sotades, and are therefore sometimes referred to as Sotadics.

Palindromic words abound, from the common, such as "civic," "noon," "tot," and "level," to the obscure, such as "Ogopogo" (a Canadian water monster), "Malayalam" (a language of South India), "Qaanaaq" (one of the northernmost naturally inhabited places on Earth, in Greenland), Harrah (in Oklahoma), and Kinnikinnik Street in Milwaukee (a Native American word referring to a mixture of bark and leaves for smoking). It is beyond conjecture that the first words ever spoken were palindromic: "Madam, I'm Adam." The longest nonobscure palindromic word in English is "redivider." A clever headline for the completion of the Panama Canal in 1920, under the supervision of Colonel G. W. Goethals of the U.S. Corps of Engineers, reads: "A man, a plan, a canal—Panama!"

Sentences can be constructed where the letters of the words, taken together, are palindromic. Of course, it is difficult to create such a palindrome that makes any sense. Consider these examples: the suggestion of diseased worms in "live dirt up a side track carted is a putrid evil!"; the provocative "harass sensuousness, Sarah!"; and the potentially heretical "dog as a devil deified, deified lived as a god."

Here are some additional palindromimic phrases, some making more sense than others: an isolated gambler (Reno loner); what some women would like to do to their sports-obsessed husbands (reflog a golfer); the punishment for a disobedient sous-chef (sit on a potato pan, Otis!); a term for old cats (senile felines); words of a patron in a Chinese restaurant upon opening a fortune cookie (egad, an adage!); statement of a second-generation member of a religious order (Ma is a nun, as I am); a grocer's request to his fresh fruit supplier (No lemons, no melon); the consequences of a canine in a Buddhist tower (A dog! A panic in a pagoda!); a Republican's comment about his opponent's campaign (star comedy by Democrats); an impossible throw of the dice (never odd or even); a swordsman's challenge (Draw, O Coward!); and a surprise for guests (party boobytrap).

Word palindromes are sentences in which the order of the words can be reversed to read the same, as in: "What? So he is dead, is he? So what?" Numbers can also be palindromic, as are the years 1991 and 2002, for example. The following date has the distinction of being palindromic, and readable right-side up or upside down, when written longhand: 10/1/01.

A word that spells another word when reversed, such as "doom," "dual," "nib," "evil," "sleek," "timer," "knits," "stressed," and "warts," is a "semordnilap." Semordnilap is an awkward word because "palindrome" is not palindromic. You can think of other semordnilaps, as did the marketers of a natural laxative, Serutan, and J. K. Rowling in the Harry Potter series, when she named a mirror that revealed the heart's desire of the viewer "Erised." If you wonder why some people pay lots of money for a small bottle of water, consider the unintended semordnilap in Evian water.

Some towns are semordnilapic, disguising words and names of people. American semordnilapic toponyms include Tesnus, Texas, Enola, Arkansas, and Egnar, Colorado. Reading backward, it is easy to find the names embedded in these Texas towns: Rolyat, Maharg, Reklaw, Sacul, and Notla. This fanciful naming extends beyond Texas's borders to Retsof, New York; Lebam, Washington; Yenruogis Park in Sigourney, Iowa; and a street in Rochester, New York, whose residents could not agree on a name: Emanon Street.

In this whole family of palindromes and semordnilaps, the most remarkable is "mom": it works as a word, a palindrome, a semordnilap, left to right and right to left, right side up, upside down, and, in the mirror, both right side up and upside down. Although just a linguistic coincidence, this is a tribute to the versatility of all the moms in the world, about whom we can only say in admiration: WOW!

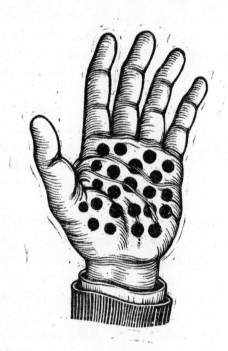

palm | polka dot

The concept of flatness, and its corollary concepts of spread out, smooth, and without rough edges, underlie a family of words based on Indo-European root *pelə-, meaning "flat." Most obvious are our words "floor" and "field"—but not "flat," which derives from Indo-European *plat- (to spread), source of such words as flan, flounder (the flat fish), piazza, plate, plateau, and plan (originally with reference to laying out the ground plan of a building).

From Latin *planus,* meaning "smooth," which derives from *pelə-,* we derive plain, plane (the mathematician's two-dimensional surface, the carpenter's smoothing tool, and what a hydroplane does on the water and an airplane does in the air), explain (figuratively, smoothing out the rough edges of understanding), and palm (referring both to the flat inner part of the hand and the flat fronds of palm trees and palm plants).

From Greek *plássein,* meaning "to spread out, mold," we derive plaster, plastic, and plasma. Plasma, the fluid portion of blood, lymph, or intramuscular fluid in which cells are suspended, is so named because of its tendency to assume the shape of its container. When celestial orbs spread out around a central star, we call them "planets," from Greek *planâsthai,* meaning "to wander, spread out."

Also derived from *pelə-* are the Slavic word for field, *polje,* and the Polish word for woman, *Polka,* female counterpart to the Polish word *Polak.* The dance we know of as the polka originated as a Czech peasant dance of Bohemian origin, and was introduced in Prague in 1831. It quickly spread throughout Europe, including England. The word for the dance likely evolved from the word for the woman with whom one danced, although it may derive from the Czech word *pulka,* meaning "half," with reference to the half-steps in the original dance. It is possible that both words contributed to the name of the dance, a happy confluence of *pulka* and *Polka* as feminine of *Polak.*

When this dance craze spread to the United States in the 1880s, clothes and designs were named after the dance. A close-fitting dot-patterned knitted jacket, suitable for dancing the polka, was called a "polka." The first recorded use of the word "polka dot" was in 1884.

panacea | pandemonium

Ubiquitousness is a versatile concept, which comes in handy in a variety of contexts. Derived from Greek *pan,* meaning "all," our "pan-" words include "pandemic," a widespread disease, "panacea," its counterpart cure-all, and such inclusionary terms as the Pan-American Games. When twentieth-century Austrian composer Arnold Schönberg developed atonal music including all twelve tones of the scale (including the sharps and flats) on an equal basis, he called it "pantonality." A pangram is a sentence using all the letters in the alphabet: "The quick brown fox jumps over the lazy dog." Two more efficient examples are: "Few quips galvanized the mock jury box." "Pack my box with five dozen liquor jugs."

"Pandemonium," meaning "a very noisy place, wild uproar or noise," literally means "all demons." Milton coined this word in 1667. In *Paradise Lost,* Pandemonium was the palace Satan built as the central part of hell. Milton derived the second element of this word from Late Latin *daemonium,* meaning "evil spirit," which evolved from Greek *daímōn,* meaning "lesser god; the power controlling the destiny of individuals," and *daimónion,* meaning "divine power." Ambrose Bierce had his own sarcastic definition of "pandemonium": "Literally, the Place of All the Demons. Most of them have escaped into politics and finance."

parallel | paramecium

The Greek word *para* had a cluster of related meanings, including "beside, near, beyond, resembling, and beside the mark." In compound words, the Greeks combined this useful word with others that evolved to create words we commonly use today, as well as many esoteric words. This "para" should not be confused with Latin *parare,* meaning "to prepare, protect against," source of such words as paramedic, paratrooper, parapet, parasol, and parade (originally, stopping to prepare).

Greek *para* combined with *allélois* (each other) is the source of Greek *parállēlos* and our word "parallel," which literally means "beside each other." When two sets of parallel lines intersect they produce a parallelogram, derived from Greek *grammé* (line). A related word is "parallax," the apparent displacement of an observed object due to a change in position of the observer, a word based on the same root as "parallel." "Paramecium," the one-celled animal with an oblong body, combines *para* with *mêkos* (length), literally, long on one side.

Other common words that are combinations with "para" are "paradigm," from *deiknynai* (to show, point out), which produced Greek verb *paradeiknynai* (to show side by side), and the Greek noun *parádeigma* (pattern). Our "paradigm" is the example or pattern for others to follow and, in geometry, a set of forms, all of which contain a particular element. A "paranormal" event, such as a fortune-teller predicting the future using such powers, or a person being abducted by space aliens, is beyond our normal experience.

Para combined with *pherne* (dowry) produced Greek *parápherna,* meaning the personal property the law allowed a woman to keep after marriage. In Latin, this word became *parapherna,* meaning "bride's property," and our "paraphernalia," meaning sundry personal belongings.

Para combined with *sîtos* (grain, food) produced Greek *parásitos,* in ancient Greece a term for a person who received free meals in return for amusing or impudent conversation. A "parasite" is any plant or animal that lives in or on an organism of another species, from which it obtains nutriment.

Still more words from Greek *para* include parameter, an independent variable in equations (*métron* means "measure"); paragraph (*gráphein* means "to write"); parenthesis (*tithénai* means "put, place"); parody (*ōidé* means "song"); paraphrase (*phrázein* means "tell, explain"); paralysis (*lýein* means "loosen, untie"); paraplegia (*pléssein* means "to strike"); and paroxysm (*oxýnein* means "sharpen, make acute"). Paraprofessionals, including paralegals, work beside the professionals they assist.

Para combined with Greek *bolé* (a throwing, casting, and source of "ballistics") produced the Greek word *parabolé,* meaning "a placing side by side, comparison, analogy," which evolved into a group of conceptually related words. A parabola is an eliptical shape based on a set of points equidistant from a fixed line and a fixed point. A parable conveys meaning by use of comparison and analogy.

Other words are less obviously related to Greek *parabolē*, which evolved into Latin *parabola,* meaning "speech or discourse," then French *parole,* specifically referring to a "formal promise," and our word "parole," which in English originally referenced a prisoner of war's word of honor not to escape. Latin *parabola* also evolved to Old French *parler* (to speak), Middle French *parlée,* and English "parley," meaning "conference to discuss disputed matters." Doublets of "parley" are parlance, parliament, and parlor.

The meaning of "parlor" (variously spelled over the centuries) expanded over time. Before 1200, "parlur" was a window through which one made confession. Around 1300, "parlour" was a conference chamber or sitting room (our "parlor" room in a house). Not until the nineteenth century did "parlor" refer to a commercial establishment, such as an ice cream, beauty, tattoo, or funeral parlor, and the parlor car on a train.

A fancy word for a pun is "paronomasia," from Greek *para* and *onomazein,* "to name." The humor in a pun derives from the juxtaposition of two words. For example, there is some humor in defining "diagnostic" as someone who doesn't believe in two gods, or "ambidextrous" as someone who takes two lumps of sugar in coffee, because of the implied juxtaposition of "diagnosis" and "di-agnostic" in the first instance, and "dexterous" and "dextrose" in the second.

There is paronomastic humor in these questions: If a pig loses its voice, is it disgruntled? Why is the man who invests all your money called a broker? If lawyers are disbarred and clergymen defrocked, why doesn't it follow that electricians can be delighted, musicians denoted, cowboys deranged, models deposed, and tree surgeons debarked? Or why can't mourners be decried, hairdressers distressed, dry cleaners depressed, examiners detested, orchestra conductors disconcerted, and swearers discussed?

Likewise, such juxtaposition is the source of humor in this joke: Man: "You know, as a stamp collector, I've accumulated quite a lot of stamps with drawings of women, but none as beautiful as you." Woman: "Philately will get you nowhere."

patter | paternity

Whether the rapid speech of an auctioneer, carnival barker, glib comedian, or rap star, there is one word to describe it: "patter." Even though "patter" sounds onomatopoetic, unlike "pitter-patter" (as in the pitter-patter of little feet), it is not. The rapid chatter that is patter may sound like "patter patter patter," but the word "patter" has religious rather than imitative roots.

When people spoke Old English, the Lord's Prayer was recited in Latin. Few people knew what they were saying, and so the Lord's Prayer, which began with the words "Pater noster" ("our Father"), was often recited rapidly and mechanically. As early as the year 900, the Lord's Prayer was referred to as "Pater Noster," and by 1175 it was spelled *paternoster*. By the fourteenth century, from the first component of this word evolved the word *patren*, meaning to mumble prayers rapidly and, more generally, to talk rapidly and easily, resulting in our word "patter." Today, rap songs are a form of patter, although they typically have nothing to do with religion.

Another possible example of a Latin prayer becoming a secular word is "hocus pocus." This magician's incantation may be an alteration of Latin *hoc est corpus meum*, which means "this is my body," the words used in the Eucharist at the time of transubstantiation in the Roman Catholic mass.

According to the venerable *Oxford English Dictionary*, "The notion that hocus pocus was a parody of the Latin words used in the Eucharist rests merely on a conjecture thrown out by Tillotson." That conjecture, in 1694, was that "in all probability those common juggling words of *hocus pocus* are nothing else but a corruption of *hoc est corpus*, by way of ridiculous imitation of the priests of the Church of Rome in their trick of Transubstantiation."

Another theory is that "hocus pocus" derived from a famous seventeenth-century conjurer who, while doing his tricks, incanted: *Hocus pocus, tontus talontus, vade celeriter jubeo*. This Latin gibberish was described by Thomas Ady in 1656 as "a dark composure of words, to blind the eyes of the beholders, to make his Trick pass the more currantly without discovery." This conjurer dubbed himself "Hocus Pocus." It may very well be that Hocus Pocus derived his name, and his phony Latin, from the perversion of *hoc est corpus meum.*

We do know that many Tudor conjurors called themselves Hocus Pocus, Hocas Pocas, Hokos Pokos, or the like, after their renowned predecessor, known for his feats of illusion and legerdemain. From "hocus pocus" we derive "hoax" and "hokum." "Hokum" is a portmanteau word, combining "hocus pocus" and "bunkum." For more on portmanteau words, see portmanteau/mantle.

Latin *pater,* the first element of *paternoster,* derives from Indo-European root *pəter-, meaning "father." Words derived from this root include father and forefather, padre, paternal, patrician, patrimony (inheritance from a father), patron, patronage, patronize, expatriate, perpetrate, patriot, patriotic, patriarch, and patronymic.

A patronymic is a name derived from the name of one's father or of a paternal ancestor. Different societies evolved a variety of surnames to perpetuate the father's name. Obvious examples are *s* at the end of a surname (e.g., Williams, Rogers, Phillips, and Peters) and "-son" at the end of a surname (e.g., "Samson" and "Thompson," both of which are on the roll call of the *Mayflower*). The name John spawned a variety of surnames, including Johns, Jonson, Johnson, Jonstone, Jenkins, Jenks, Jones, Jennings, and Jackson. (John, and nickname Jack, also produced a host of common words, which you will find in jacket/jack-o'-lantern.)

Other examples include Irish "O'" (as in American painter Georgia O'Keeffe); Scottish and Gaelic "Mc" and Mac" (as in American general Douglas MacArthur); Arabic "ibn" (as in the names of tenth-century scientist Abu Ali al-Hasan ibn al-Haytham, the founder of modern optics, and fourteenth-century Arab historian ibn-Khaldun) and "bin" (as in Osama bin Laden); Hebrew "ben" (as in Ben-Hur and the name of Polish-born David Gruen who, when he moved to Palestine and before becoming the first prime minister of Israel, changed his name to David Ben-Gurion); Norman "Fitz" (as in American writer F. Scott Fitzgerald and American Olympic speed skater Casey FitzRandolph); Spanish "-ez" (as in baseball player Alex Rodriguez, and names such as Fernandez and Gonzalez); Hindi "-putra" (as in Brahmaputra, son of Brahma, and Rajput, son of a king); Welsh "ap" or "p" (as in Pritchard, from "ap Richard"); Slavonic "-vitch" (as in Solomon Rabinovich, better known as writer Sholom Aleichem); Teutonic "-sohn" (as in Felix Mendelssohn); Turkish "-oglu"; Italian "Di"; and use of "Jr." or "II" after a surname.

Vlad, a fifteenth-century Romanian, changed his name to Dracul (meaning "the dragon") when he joined an organization called "the Order of the Dragon." Vlad's son took the name for himself, tacking on the patronymic "a." Dracula was a very real figure from Romanian history.

A variation on this theme is the use of "-dottir" as a suffix in women's surnames in Scandinavian countries and in Iceland. For example, a former president of Iceland is Vigdis Finnbogadóttir and the patronymic of Icelandic pop idol Bjork is Gudmundsdottir. The use of this form of patronymic reflects the fact that, even centuries ago, Icelandic women could own land, control family finances, and divorce husbands, whose names they never took. Our enlightened way of dealing with this issue is to take on hyphenated names after marriage, as when Roger Throckmorton marries Alice Prendergast, and they both take on the surname Throckmorton-Prendergast. This can be a source of some confusion.

In England, heirs of estates were sometimes compelled by the terms of a will to adopt the surnames of the families whose property they inherited, resulting in double-barreled, and, on occasion, triple-barreled names. Such actual surnames include "Uniacke-Penrose-FitzGerald," "Mainwaring-Synnerton-Pilkington," and "Dillwyn-Venables-Llewelyn." Some surnames were even longer, including the improbable "Temple-Nugent-Chandos-Brydges-Grenville."

Perplexing patronymic problems can arise from other attempts to perpetuate a father's name. For example, in Sweden, the eighteen most common names end in "son," including almost 300,000 Johanssons, and the Stockholm phone book lists forty-eight *pages* of Anderssons. In Denmark, where identical names are more common than anywhere else in Europe, almost one in four Danes is called Jensen, Hansen, or Nielsen, and two-thirds of the population has a surname ending in "sen." Mistaken identity is a way of life in phone calls, public paging, mail and package deliveries, and, with potentially more dire consequences, in surgical wards.

American boxer George Foreman has his own way of distinguishing his sons George, Jr., George 3rd, George 4th, and George 5th: by their nicknames. If you are wondering, the formidable and fertile Foreman also has four daughters, only one of whom he named Georgetta—the others have non-Georgean names Michi, Freeda, and Natalie.

In a 1988 interview, Mr. Foreman explained his patronymic practice, expressing a motivation that underlies patronymics in all societies: "One of the baddest feelings I had was that feeling of not knowing where I came from, what my roots were. I figured that with all of them having that name, they should know where they come from. It's never too late to get some roots."

pavilion | fold

If you think about butterflies, you'll see the connection between these two words. "Pavilion" derives from Latin *papilio, papilionis,* meaning "butterfly" and "tent." The sense of "tent" derives from the resemblence of a tent to a butterfly with outstretched wings. To protect against the elements, the ancient Romans stretched a multi-hued cloth, like an awning, over upright poles. This cloth structure, when opened, looked like a giant butterfly with wings spanning outward. For a similar animalistic development, see the etymology of "muscle" in muscle/mouse.

These temporary structures became popular in France, where they were called, in Old French, *paveillon, pavilloun,* or *pavilun,* evolving in the seventeenth century to our frequently misspelled word "pavilion" for an ornate tent, light roofed structure, or arena.

Uncommon but related words are papillon (a breed of small dog with ears shaped like the wings of a butterfly), papillote (the frilled paper cover used to decorate the bone end of a cooked chop or cutlet), and papilionaceous (a plant having bilaterally symmetrical petals resembling a butterfly).

Some etymologists believe that Latin *papilio* is of unknown origin, but others believe it derives from Indo-European *pel-, meaning "to fold." If you ever watched the way a butterfly folds its wings to become a nearly two-dimensional object, a primary feature of a butterfly is its ability to fold itself flat. (Compare the etymology of dodo, squirrel, lynx, and reindeer, all named for their primary features, discussed in canary/cynic, carrot/hornet, and lunatic/lynx.) From *pel- we derive such words as fold, manifold, multiple, octuple, diploid, triple, and the mellifluous word furbelow (a ruffle or flounce on a garment).

All these words relate to butterflies, but none means "butterfly," unlike French, in which the word for butterfly is *papillon.* The origin of "butterfly" is obscure, although it is known that it derives from Old English *butorfleoge,* a compound of words meaning "butter" and "fly." It is not a reversal of "flutter-by." At least four theories, some more fanciful than others, seek to provide the derivation: (1) according to medieval folklore, fairies and witches in the form of butterflies (rather than midnight snackers) stole butter in the dark of night; (2) it was once believed that butterflies landed on and consumed milk or butter left uncovered in the kitchen or dairy (compare the German word for butterfly, *Milchdieb,* literally "milk thief"); (3) the word derives from the yellow color of some butterfly species; and (4) a butterfly's excrement is the color of butter (the least appetizing theory).

pedigree | crane

Medieval genealogists used a three-line symbol, like an upside-down Y, to denote the line of descent of families. A medieval scholar observed that this figure resembled the imprint of the crane's foot.

In French, the court language of many kingdoms, "foot of the crane" was *pied de grue*. This term came to refer to the genealogical symbol and for the line of descent itself. In the fifteenth century, *pied de grue* joined the English lexicon in variant forms "pee de grew," "petiegrew," and "peti degree," and, ultimately, as our "pedigree."

Pied de grue derives from Latin *pes* (foot) and *grus* (crane). *Pes*, genitive *pedis*, is the source of such words as pedal, pedestrian, pedestal, pedicure, and impede. *Grus* is the source of "crane" for both the bird and the device for lifting, which resembles the bird. *Grus* is also the source of "geranium," so named for the long pointed "beak" of its fruit, and "cranberry," for its beaklike stamens.

poem | onomatopoeia

The act of creation unites these two words. Etymologically, a "poem" is something created, a word derived from Greek *poieîn* meaning "make, create." In ancient Greece, this word signified any artist— whether musician, painter, or writer—each of whom made forms that do not exist in nature. The original sense of "something created" developed metaphorically to refer to the literary work we know of as a "poem" (via Greek *póēma*, Latin *poema*, and Old French *poeme*), written by a poet (via Greek *pōetḗs*, and Latin *poeta*).

Shakespeare captures the creativity of poetry in this line from *A Midsummer Night's Dream*:

> . . . as imagination bodies forth
> The forms of things unknown, the poet's pen
> Turns them to shapes, and gives to airy nothing
> A local habitation and a name.

John Donne likewise defines poetry as "a counterfeit creation, and makes things that are not, as though they were."

Poieîn is also the root for "pharmacopoeia," the druggist's collection of drugs and "prosopopoeia," a figure of speech in which an inanimate object or abstraction is endowed with human qualities or represented as possessing human form. We engage in prosopopoeia whenever we say "mother nature," "father time," or such adages as "necessity is the mother of invention." Shelley employed prosopopoeia when he wrote: "bask in Heaven's blue smile," as did Johann Christoph Friedrich von Schiller in his ode "To Joy" (familiar to anyone who has heard the rousing finale of Beethoven's Ninth Symphony): "All creatures drink of Joy . . . Follow in her rose-strewn wake. She gave us kisses and vines, And a friend who has proved faithful even in death."

"Onomatopoeia," a word in imitation of a sound, derives from the same Greek root, *poieîn*. Literally, an onomatopoeia is a name that is made up. "Onomato-" derives from *ónoma*, Greek for "name." The word *ónoma* is the root for our alphabet soup of "-onym" words, such as acronym, antonym, eponym, heteronym, homonym, patronym, pseudonym, retronym, synonym, toponym, and zoonym.

The word *ónoma* is based on the same Indo-European root (*nomen-) that evolved into such "name" words as anonymous, nominal, nominate, denominate, nominative, noun, pronoun, misnomer, renown, ignominy, moniker, cognomen (a surname), and "name" itself. One unlikely *nomen- word is the name for Nome, Alaska. When a coastal survey chart was being prepared, this point along the Alaskan coast had no name. A London draftsman carelessly copied the name of this location, written "? Name"—indicating that the name was unknown—as "Point Nome."

Some poetry is overtly onomatopoetic, as in Tennyson's mellifluous lines from "Come Down, O Maid," which must be read aloud: "The moan of doves in immemorial elms / And murmuring of innumerable bees." Mellifluous onomatopoeias include babbling, coo, tweet, chirp, swish, strum, purr, and tintinnabulation. But most onomatopoeias are cacophonous, such as bang, buzz, click, peekaboo, ticktock, splat, sizzle, twitter, twang, kerplunk, whoosh, and zoom. Some words are not obviously onomatopoetic, such as "clock," which entered the lexicon in the fourteenth century, when the hours were sounded by bells. (A doublet for "clock" is "glockenspiel," a percussion instrument having tuned bells or bars, assembled on a frame.)

For a treasure trove of onomatopoeias, read the comics. The most memorable cartoon-inspired onomatopoeias were the product of the wildly zany imagination of *Mad* magazine cartoonist Don Martin, whom the *New York Times* described as having "elevated the comic book sound effect to new onomatopoetic heights." In his wacky world, a squirting flower went "SHKLITZA." Getting slapped in the face with a wet mackerel went "SPLADAP," while getting conked with a frying pan went "PWANG." Don Martin's caco-phanous vanity plate was "SHTOINK."

We name birds onomatopoetically, for their chirps, tweets, and calls. Thus we have named the whippoorwill, nightingale (from *naht meaning "night" and *galon meaning "sing," source of "yell" and "yelp"), chickadee, cockatoo (from Malay *kakatua* via Dutch *kaketoe*), pigeon (from Latin *pipiare* meaning "to chirp," source of "pipe," as in "pipe organ"), and cuckoo (for the bird's monotonous call).

Less obviously onomatopoetic is "swan," from Indo-European *swen-, and Old English *swinsian,* meaning "sing." This apparently anomalous name is explained by the fact that it originally referred to the European whooper swan, rather than its more common relative, the mute swan. The term "swan song," for a person's last piece of work or performance, derives from the ancient Greek myth that the mute swan, just before death, sings a song of unsurpassed beauty. According to this legend, the song was joyous, because the dying bird, sacred to Apollo, knew it would soon join its master. This term is a loan translation from the German *Schwanengesang.*

We don't all hear onomatopoetic animal sounds the same way. For example, our version of the cock's crow ("cock-a-doodle-doo") is heard as *cocorico* (French), *chichirichi* (Italian), *quiquiriqui* (Spanish), *kikerike* (German), *kukuriku* (Russian), *kong-shi* (Chinese), and *kokekoko* (Japanese). Our pig's "oink" is *groin* (French), *gru* (Italian), *tru* (Spanish), *quiek* (German), *kroo* (Russian), *oh-ee* (Chinese), and *bu* (Japanese).

Onomatopoeias may explain the origin of language. According to one theory of the evolution of language, known as the "bow-wow" theory, the first speech was imitative of animal sounds, as a means of identifying them. This type of speech is noticeable in a child's reference to a bovine as a "moo-cow," a canine as a "bow-wow," and the expression "baa-baa black sheep." The word for cat in Chinese is *mao*, spoken in imitation of the cat's meow.

Even today, we apply the same aural logic when we say the word "barbarian." In expanding their civilization, the Greeks encountered people who spoke "foreign" languages. In imitation of the unintelligible speech of these people, the Greeks dubbed them *bárbaros* (from imitative "bar-bar-bar"), a word that originally meant "stammering," then acquired the meanings "rude" and "foreign." The ultimate signification of *bárbaros* may have been "unable to speak intelligibly," a conclusion buttressed by the fact that the related Sanskrit *barbara-s* meant "stammering." A *vox barbara* is a barbarous word or phrase, especially applied to supposedly neo-Latin terms that are neither Latin nor Greek. The feminine of *bárbaros* is the source of the name for any woman named "Barbara," even if she is articulate. In a related onomatopoetic development, the medical term for the stomach's rumblings is "borborygmi."

Derisively echoic *bárbaros* evolved to our words barbarian, brave, bravo, and rhubarb, a plant which proliferated along the Volga River when it was known as the Rha River. In Greek, this plant was known as *rhâ bárbaron* because it was a foreign plant from the region of the Rha River. This name became *rha barbarum* in medieval Latin, and our "rhubarb."

portmanteau | mantle

In modern English, a portmanteau is a traveling bag with two compartments. In Middle French, this same word referred to the officer who carried a prince's mantle. This appropriately compound word is based on the imperative form of Old French *porter* (to carry), and *manteau* (cloak, from Latin *mantellum,* meaning "mantle"). A mantle is a loose, sleeveless coat worn over an outer garment, like a cloak.

Charles Lutwidge Dodgson, whose pen name was Lewis Carroll, was the first to use "portmanteau" as a noun to describe the blending of two words into one, for such coinages as his "slithy" (lithe and slimy) and the very useful "chortle," a blend of chuckle and snort. Within a decade, "portmanteau" had become an adjective for such words. Carroll relies on Humpty-Dumpty to explain to Alice (and to the reader) what "slithy" means, in *Through the Looking Glass, and What Alice Found There,* written in 1871. Alice repeats the first verse of "Jabberwocky":

> 'Twas brillig, and the slithy toves
> Did gyre and gimble in the wabe;
> All mimsy were the borogroves,
> And the mome raths outgrabe.

Humpty-Dumpty explains: "Well, 'slithy' means 'lithe and slimy.' 'Lithe' is the same as 'active.' You see it's like a portmanteau—there are two meanings packed up into one word." "I see it now," Alice remarked thoughtfully . . ."

Our lexicon abounds with portmanteau words, including motel (motor and hotel); brunch (breakfast and lunch); electrocute (electricity and execute); heliport (helicopter and airport); smog (smoke and fog); advertorial (advertisement and editorial); infomercial (information and commercial); nutriceutical (nutrient and pharmaceutical); Chunnel (channel and tunnel); slanguage (slang and language); Franglais (French and Anglais); Breathalyzer (breath and analyzer); affluenza (affluence and influenza, the malady suffered by the superrich); dockominium (dock and condominium); flabbergasted (flabby and aghast); threepeat (three and repeat); labradoodle (a mix of Labrador retriever and poodle); netiquette (Internet and etiquette), emoticon (emotion and icon, like ☺); Webinar (an online seminar), kubris (geek-speak for extreme arrogance of multimedia auteurs who think they are Stanley Kubrick); and bodacious (bold and audacious). Even a person's name can be portmanteau-ized: Pulitzer Prize winner Herbert Lawrence Block was known to readers of his *Washington Post* editorial cartoons as "Herblock."

Portmanteau words provide endless opportunities for inventiveness. In Las Vegas, where shopping is rivaling gambing as a principal attraction, one of the casinos expanded what it dubbed its "streetmosphere" program by adding mimes, jugglers, strolling opera singers, and the like. "Tofurky" is a registered trademark for the vegetarian's solution to deal with Thanksgiving, advertised as good news for vegetarians and turkeys. Turkey-free, it is a blend of tofu, tempeh, and wheat protein.

More fanciful portmanteau words include "Cocacolonization" for the idea that a country has been taken over by American values; the bumper sticker admonition "Don't Californicate Oregon"; and the warm and fuzzy "I LOVERMONT."

Some towns bordering other countries or other states are portmanteau-ized. Calexico is across the border from Mexicali. Any student of U.S. political geography can readily figure out the locations of Calzona, PenMar, Kenvir, Kensee, Kanorado, Virgilina, Moark, Illmo, Arkla, Texhoma, Florala, Idavada, Tennga, Monida, Texarkana, and Kenova (somewhat obscure, it is located on the borders of Kentucky, Ohio, and West Virginia).

A most prolific source of portmanteau words is the Watergate Hotel in Washington, D.C., site of the infamous 1972 break-in by agents of Nixon's infelicitously named CREEP (Committee to Re-Elect the President), source of the name for what was immediately dubbed the "Watergate" scandal. The suffix "-gate" is like a snap-on Lego piece, easily attached to almost any prefix. The Watergate scandal was so momentous that it opened the floodgates to a spate of "-gate" portmanteau words.

Since 1972, any attempted cover-up or scandal is a good candidate for a "-gate" eponymous portmanteau neologism, such as Volgagate (Russian scandal); Motorgate (fraud inquiry at General

Motors); Oilgate (British North Sea oil scandal); Billygate (scandal over Libyan connections of Jimmy Carter's brother); Altergate (allegations that transcripts of official hearings in the United States had been altered); Contragate and Irangate (the Iran-contra affair); Pearlygate (the scandal involving televangelists—itself a portmanteau word); and Andersengate (the infamous shredding of Enron documents).

The public loves scandals, and reporters are resourceful in conjuring up more "-gate" words to describe them. A Polish scandal involving a black market in goods was dubbed "Schnappsgate"; a scandal involving a congressman's abuse of check-cashing privileges was "Rubbergate." The story of a submarine accident in 1992, news of which the former USSR had repressed, surfaced as (what else?) "Underwatergate."

Have some fun and make up your own portmanteau words—call them "twords" if you like. J. K. Rowling did so in the Harry Potter books with such neologisms as "Animagus" for a wizard who could be transformed into an animal—a blend of "animal" and "magus" (a magician). You could invent a word for the length of time between stepping on a banana peel and hitting the ground—a "bananosecond."

Especially challenging are portmanteau words that include every letter of the root words, such as "palimony," the equivalent of alimony but without benefit of marriage. This word was coined in the late 1970s, when the live-in girlfriend of actor Lee Marvin sued him after they broke up, ending what the court judiciously referred to as "an unsolemnized relationship." See bully/friar for more on "pal."

Here are some neologistic portmanteau words, all retaining intact the root words. The last four meld three words, even though the original portmanteau traveling bag had only two compartments:

cameow (the brief appearance of a cat in a movie)

squarea (the length times the width of a right-angled rhombus)

devilest (the most wicked demon)

twelves (a dozen sprites)

neighbourgeois (a middle-class person who lives next door in London)

policense (the authority to arrest for a crime)

cloudest (the nearest thunderclap)

sevents (the acts of creation, including the day of rest)

lostrich (a disoriented large flightless bird)

Myanmarriage (a wedding in the former Burma)

widowagerer (a rich betting woman whose husband has died)

impenduluminescence (a swinging light about to smash into something)

peasantiquest (a search for old domestic items of value once used by a rustic country person)

limbroglion (a fiasco when the roaring animal bit someone's arm)

precocious | apricot

The first syllable of "precocious" derives from Latin *prae*, meaning "before." This useful prefix appears in numerous words, including the more obvious preheat, predict, preamble, and precedent, and the less obvious pretense, prevail, pregnant, and preposterous. "Preposterous" literally means "with the last" (*posterus*) coming "first" (*prae*).

The second syllable of "precocious" derives from Latin *coquere*, meaning "to cook" and, metaphorically, "to ripen." Latin *praecoquere* meant either "to cook in advance" or "to ripen in advance." A Latin derivative of *praecoquere* was *praecox*, genitive *praecocis*. *Praecox* survives today in the term "dementia praecox," referring to schizophrenia, a presenile form of mental disorder. "Precocious" joined the English lexicon in the seventeenth century, and refers to any prematurely developed faculty, whether applied to a child displaying talents earlier than normal or a tree producing early ripened fruit.

"Apricot" likewise derives from *praecox,* by a far-flung route. The original term the Romans used for this fruit, which ultimately is a native of China, was *prunum Arminiacum* ("Armenian plum") or *malum Arminiacum* ("Armenian apple"), because Armenia, which once extended over what is now part of Turkey, was a source of choice apricots. Even today, the botanical term for the apricot is *Prunus armeniaca.*

The apricot ripens earlier in the season than other fruits, and so the Romans also referred to this fruit as *praecoquis* or *praecoquum.* This word traveled across the Mediterranean, becoming in Byzantine Greek *praikókion,* with variants *berikókkon* and plural *berikókkia.* By trade and Ptolemaic influence in Arabic culture, apricots and the Greek word for them were transported to southwestern Europe during the time of Moslem domination of Spain. The Arabic word for this fruit, from the Greek, was *al-barquq,* the first syllable meaning "the." For other words derived from Arabic "al-," see alcohol/artichoke.

Arabic *al-barquq* evolved into Catalan *abaercoc,* Spanish *albaricoque,* and Portuguese *albricoque.* This word entered English as "abrecock" in the sixteenth century, but by the seventeenth century, the spelling had evolved into "apricot." The change from "*b*" to "*p*" may be from the influence of Latin *apricus,* meaning "sunny" (the obscure word *apricate* once meant "to bask in the sun"), and the change from "-cock" to "-cot" may be from influence of French *abricot* for apricot, or merely one more instance of prudery, by elimination of "cock" and similar words in our lexicon, even if making their disapproved appearance only as syllables. For more on such euphemisms, see brassiere/pretzel.

The ultimate source for Latin *coquere,* the source of the third syllable of "apricot," is Indo-European *pekw-, meaning "to cook, ripen." Derivatives of *pekw- include cook, culinary, kitchen, cuisine, ricotta (from Italian, via Latin *recocta,* cooked again), biscuit (originally a soldier's or sailor's ration, cooked twice to dry for storage), and cookie.

But *pekw- words are not limited to the kitchen. A "cookie" in geek speak is a tiny file containing information about computers that can be used by advertisers to track users' online interests and tastes. A kiln heats clay to make pottery, and terra-cotta, literally "baked earth," is a ceramic clay used in pottery and building construction.

When we cook up a scheme together, we "concoct" it, from Latin *concoquere*, to boil together. Picture the witches in act IV of Shakespeare's *Macbeth*, hunched over the boiling cauldron, concocting "a charm of powerful trouble" by their mischievous gruel consisting of eye of newt, toe of frog, wool of bat, tongue of dog, scale of dragon, tooth of wolf, nose of Turk, Tartar's lips, and baboon's blood (to name just a few of their choice ingredients), while incanting: "Double, double toil and trouble; Fire burn and cauldron bubble."

*Pekw- evolved into Greek *péptein* (soften or ripen), whence the pepsin the stomach produces to digest proteins; peptic ulcers; and pumpkins (originally a kind of melon eaten only when wholly ripe). Via Sanskrit, *pekw- evolved into Hindi *pukka*, meaning "cooked, ripe, mature," Anglo-Indian *pukka* meaning "genuine, reliable, or good," and *pukka sahib*, a term of respectful address formerly used by natives of India when addressing British colonial authorities.

quarry | squadron

In common experience, things aren't often grouped in nines, elevens, or seventeens, for example; but things are often grouped in fours, giving rise to a number of four-based words. Indo-European root *kwetwer-, meaning four, is the root of such words as four, fourth, forty, fourteen, and farthing (one-fourth of a penny), all via Old English; square, via Latin *quadrum* (square); quadrant, via Latin *quadrans* (fourth-part); and quart, quarter, quarto, quatrain (a stanza or poem of four lines), and quadroon (having one-fourth black ancestry), all via Latin *quattuor* (four) and *quartus* (fourth, quarter).

The "fourness" of things is not as obvious in other words based on *kwetwer-. The carillon, for example, is a set of chromatically tuned bells in a tower, usually played from a keyboard, for a mellifluous effect more soothing than church bells. The original carillon consisted of a set of four bells hung in the tower of a church, and so derived its name from Late Latin *quaternion*, via Old French *quarregnon*, meaning "by fours."

People as well as things are sometimes grouped in fours. A nucleus of trained personnel around which a larger organization can be built, or a tightly knit group of zealots, is a "cadre," from Latin *quadrum* (square), via Italian *quadro*. A small group of people organized in a common endeavor, and the smallest tactical unit of military personnel or police officers, is a "squad," from Vulgar Latin *exquadra* (square). A "squadron," then, is a military unit based on the same word root.

The same square sense is in "quarry," the usually square-shaped open excavation from which stone is obtained, and the process by which stone or information is obtained, derived from Latin *quadrum*. Other words in this *quadrum* family are quadrille, a square dance of French origin and a card game for four people popular in the eighteenth century, and quarrel, meaning both a tool with a squared head and a square pane of glass in a latticed window. "Quarrel," meaning "argument," is not based on four. After all, it only takes two people to quarrel. That "quarrel" is based on Latin *guerella* (complaint), appropriately from Indo-European root *kwes- (to pant or wheeze, source of our word "wheeze").

A quarantine is a period of time during which someone or something suspected of carrying a contagious disease is detained at a port of entry to prevent the disease from entering the country or, more generally, any period of enforced isolation. While the period of quarantine may vary, this word derives from the idea that the period of quarantine is forty days, from Latin *quadraginta* (forty), via Italian *quaranta (giorni)*, and *quarantina*, meaning forty (days).

Cater-corner, the first component of which is variously spelled cata-, catta-, catter-, catti-, catty-, caddy-, cally-, caper-, cat-, kitter-, and katter-, and in the American South, spelled catawampuws and cattywampus, literally means "four-cornered." This useful word principally means diagonal but has taken on the ancillary meanings of out of line or out of sorts. It derives from Latin *quattuor* (four), via Old French *catre* (four).

Indo-European *kwetwer- evolved into Greek *tetra* (four) and such words as tetrad (a group of four), tetrahedron (a polyhedron with four faces), and Tetragrammaton (the four Hebrew letters for the name of God, usually transliterated as YHWH or JHVH, letters spelling Yahweh and Jehovah).

quintessence | fist

Twenty-six centuries ago, Greek philosopher Thales reasoned that all matter must be formed from a single element: water. Other Greeks in Thales's time believed that the single source element was either air, fire, or earth. Greek philosopher Empedocles combined these ideas, espousing the theory that all matter is made up of these four elements. Aristotle added a fifth element, which permeates all things and forms the substance of the heavenly bodies, which he called *aithér* (our word ether).

Ancient Greeks also referred to the *aithér* of Aristotle as *pémptē ousiā,* the "fifth essence," a term that by loan translation became *quinta essentia* in medieval Latin. (*Quinta* is the feminine of *quintus,* meaning "fifth.") The word "quintessence" entered our modern lexicon in the fifteenth century as "quyntessense," via Middle French *quinte essence,* and acquired the metaphorical sense "most perfect or characteristic embodiment" in the sixteenth century.

By medieval times, after two thousand years of investigation, the natural elements were believed to be water, air, fire, earth, ether, mercury, sulfur, and salt. Medieval alchemists knew of other substances such as gold, silver, copper, iron, tin, lead, mercury, and carbon, but didn't recognize them as elements. We now know of at least 112 elements, named either for their characteristics or eponymously.

Even though Thales was misguided in his belief that all matter is formed from a single element, scientists today are in search for one set of equations unifying all fundamental interactions in nature, known as the unified field theory. Their objective is to provide a common explanation for gravitation, electromagnetism, and the strong and weak nuclear forces. Thus, even though scientists have so far discovered more than a hundred elements, they continue, like Thales, in their quest to discover the single unifying aspect of the universe—the quintessence of the universe's forces.

Stephen Hawking captured the essence of this search for the ultimate quintessence in *A Brief History of Time*: "If we do discover a complete [unified] theory [of the universe] . . . then we shall all, philosophers, scientists, and just ordinary people, be able to take part in the discussion of the question of why it is that we and the universe exist. If we find the answer to that, it would be the ultimate triumph of human reason—for then we should know the mind of God."

The Indo-European root for "quintessence" is *penkwe-, which evolved via Latin into quintet, quintuple, and quintillion. Americans and Brits cannot agree on the meaning of quintillion. Americans, together with Canadians and the French, define it as a cardinal number equal to ten to the eighteenth power. (There are *five* sets of three zeroes after 1,000.) The British define quadrillion as ten to the thirtieth power, because they group zeroes by sixes rather than threes. (There are *five* sets of six zeroes.) Likewise, we can't agree on the definition of a billion—a thousand million in the United States and elsewhere, but a million million in England. This discrepancy is yet another example of the truth of the adage that the United States and England are two countries divided by the same language.

From the Indo-European root "*penkwe-" we also derive five, fifth, fifteen, fifty, finger, fist, and, less obviously, foist. "Foist" derives, via Old English *fyst*, meaning "fist," from Dutch *vuisten*, to take in hand, that is, the five fingers, and *voist*, meaning "to pass off as genuine." *Penkwe- evolved, via Greek, to pentagon, pentathlon (a track and field event consisting of sprinting, hurdling, long jumping, discus, and javelin), and Pentecost.

The word "punch" for a type of mixed drink may be based on this same Indo-European root, via Sanskrit *páñca* (five) and Hindi *panch*. This alludes to the fact that the traditional Indian drink had five elements: spirits, water, lemon juice, sugar, and spice. This etymology has been disputed, however, on various grounds. One is that "punch" appeared in England *before* India fell to British rule. Even though a suggestion has been made that "punch" is an abbreviation of "puncheon" (barrel), itself a word of uncertain origin, the Indian derivation is widely cited as a possibility.

The word "punch" meaning "hit," although delivered with a fist, is unrelated to five. Instead, it derives from Latin *pungere,* meaning "to prick," source of such words as point, puncture, punctuation, pungent, and poignant. *Pungere* derives from Indo-European *peuk-, *peug-, which is also likely the source of Latin *pugnare,* meaning "to fight." *Pugnare* evolved to our words pugilist and pugnacious.

re | rebus

The word "thing" is a handy, all-purpose word to describe just about anything. Its Latin equivalent was *res*. We rely on word order to convey whether a word, such as "thing," is being used as a subject ("The thing had wings and a lion's mane"), direct object ("I put the thing in the kitchen"), indirect object ("I gave the thing a dead mouse to eat"), or object of a preposition ("That was all I could put before the thing to eat, since I had no other food suitable for what I realized was a griffin"). The ancient Romans were more versatile, using the same word anywhere in a sentence, but with different suffixes, to indicate the word's proper role in the action.

Re is the ablative of *res*. To the ancient Romans, *re* meant "in the matter of." *Rebus* is the plural ablative of *res,* used when more than one thing was the object of a preposition. "Re" is frequently used in law and commerce meaning "in the case of [a thing]," or "with reference to [a thing]," usually as a caption for a memo, as in "RE:

PROPER NUTRITION FOR GRIFFINS." When judges have jurisdiction only because a thing happens to be located within their district, and there is a squabble over who has title to it, the caption of the case is "*In re* . . ." This is called in rem jurisdiction. For example, when Panama and members of Jordan's royal family disputed ownership of a plane, the case was captioned *In re B-727 Aircraft Serial No. 21010.*

Since lawyers are always dealing with "things," many legal maxims have developed over the centuries, chock full of "res" and its variants. When a court has made a final decision, a litigant can't retry the same claim against the same adversary. Lawyers and judges call the underlying principle that precludes retrying cases already ruled upon "res judicata"—literally "the thing already decided." In international law, "rebus sic stantibus" pertains to the duration of the binding force of a treaty—for as long as the relevant facts and circumstances remain basically the same. It is pure Latin for "with things remaining thus."

"Res" is also a component of the legal maxim "Res ipsa loquitur," Latin for "the thing speaks for itself." Normally, the mere happening of an accident does not give rise to a presumption that it arose from negligence. But sometimes negligence is self-evident— "the thing speaks for itself."

This legal principle originated in several nineteenth century English cases, one of which was *Byrne v. Boadle,* decided in 1863, in which a barrel of flour rolled out of a window of an English warehouse and fell on a passing pedestrian, who sued the warehouse owner for his injuries. As the judge succinctly put it: "In my opinion the fact of its falling is prima facie evidence of negligence." Over one hundred years later in Ohio, a beer keg rolled off a platform and fell on a passing pedestrian, proving that history sometimes *does* repeat itself. The court applied the doctrine of res ipsa loquitur, citing *Byrne v. Boadle* as authority. This doctrine has been applied in many other instances in which the "thing" really does "speak for itself": fall of an elevator; derailment of a train; explosion of a boiler; and an oil spill in a harbor.

Some legal "res" terms are self-explanatory, such as res controversa, res fungibiles, res immobiles, and res religiosae, but others are not, such as res caduca (things that can be conveyed to the state by escheat), res serviens (the servient estate), and the deceptively named res universitatis (things belonging to the community, such as public buildings and streets).

"Rebus" literally means "by things," that is, something that is created by the use of things. A rebus is a representation of a word or phrase by a combination of letters, pictures, and symbols that suggest that word or phrase or its syllables. It is a shortened version of the Latin phrase *non verbis sed rebus,* which means "not by words but by things."

The earliest form of rebuses is in picture writings, common in Egyptian hieroglyphs and early Chinese pictographs. In East Asia, especially China and Korea, rebus symbols were commonly employed to carry auspicious wishes. Rebus pictures were used to convey names of towns on Greek and Roman coins. In Europe, rebuses first became popular in sixteenth-century France, probably in the province of Picardy, and were called *rébus de Picardie.* In the seventeenth century, Parisian lawyers adopted rebuses for satirizing current events without risk of legal action.

In heraldry, the coat of arms sometimes suggested the name of the family, visually making an indirect reference to a name or an incident from family history. These rebuses were known as canting arms, allusive arms, or armes parlant. For example, a lock and heart formed the name Lockhart; and an eye and a tun (cask) conveyed the name Eyeton; three pigs symbolized the name Bacon; and three old men's heads ('eads) symbolized the name Eady.

Literary rebuses often appeared on family mottoes, personal seals, ciphers, bookplates, and eventually in games and riddles. English family mottoes were sometimes puns, as in "I dare" (Adair), "Light on" (Leighton), and "Bear thee well" (Bardwell). Some of these punning mottoes were bilingual: *Ad gloriam per spinas*—"To glory through thorns" (Thorn); *Age omne bonum*—"Do all good" (Algood); and *Bene factum*—"Well done" (Weldon). In the United States, rebuses became popular as riddles and eventually provided the theme of the television show *Concentration,* which aired from 1958 to 1961.

The best vehicle, so to speak, for rebuses in modern society is the vanity plate. A memorable *New Yorker* cartoon showed a man in a sports car (license LK2XLR8) getting a ticket by a cop (license LV2TKT). There are more than a million vanity plates in California alone.

Here is a selective culling of some of the more clever rebus vanity plates from around the country: CME4DK (dentist); CU N QRT (attorney); ATY2B (paralegal); DR IIII (optometrist); TZVECL (ophthalmologist, for the letters on the eye chart); STR8NR (orthodontist); SPLAT (exterminator); PILPUSR (pharmacist); IKNEADU (massage therapist); ISD8EM (anesthesiologist); ITOETAG (coroner); 16 APR (accountant); I12BNZC (deep-sea diver); IX FE (golfer); 10SNE1 (tennis player); and NT (bridge player).

Some people use rebus vanity plates to convey a social message, as in the provocative but indiscriminate CME4AD8, RUBZ2NT, 1NTSTND, and MSAGRO; and to describe themselves as cocky (4U2NV, 2FAST4U, 2DIE4); outraged (DMV SUX); admonishing (DNTB2NR); existentialist (WHOCARZ); unhappy (PMSX365); wistful (OH2B39); shapely (GR82SH); newlywed (WED4LIFE); and not someone else (NOT OJ, on a White Bronco in California).

Other people describe their cars on vanity plates, including, for example, PRRR (on a Jaguar); PAWSH (on a Porsche), and NICE EH (on a really beat-up car). One fellow felt the need to convey to the world his special relationship to his car, which he *really* loves: CARGASM.

As you drive along, you learn how some people raised the money for their cars: MY FEE (presumably on an attorney's car); THANKXDAD; DADIOU; EZ2CYIO (on a Porsche); STOLEN (on a 1965 Corvette); NO WIFE (on a Jeep Grand Cherokee pulling a new fishing boat); TAXRFND; WON IT (on a pink Caddy); NOETHCS; and WAS HIS (on a Jaguar, presumably postdivorce).

As playful with language as the Eady family was in using "'eads" for their allusive arms, people have vanity plates that are palindromic (ATOYOTA, UNIXINU, and the urgent OGOTTOGO), puns (S5280FT—smile), and include the feminist query (H20MEN4—what are men for?); the license of a fellow named Noel (JK MNO); and a reference to Alice in Wonderland on a Volkswagen Rabbit (ML8ML8). A bakery truck has a license plate that must be understood in context: GR8BUNS. A particularly clever vanity plate appeared on a new Nissan 300 ZK (commonly referred to as a "Z") in New Jersey: NUJOYZ, capturing in a mere six letters the newness of the car, the model, the pleasure of the new owner in driving it, the state he's from, and the way he would pronounce the name of that state. Other vanity plates must be read in the rear view mirror to be understood, such as the admonition to T13VOM and, on a bakery truck, the encouragement to 3MTA3. A portent of things to come appears on a vanity plate spotted in Mendocino, California: BATTRYREQ.

For a similar development of the use of rebuses, see OK/ kindergarten.

remorse | morsel

The unifying principle here is "bite." Latin *morsus* meant "bite," from the verb *mordere*, "to bite." A morsel is something bitten off, and remorse is the conscience that "bites" again and again, from Latin *remorsus*, meaning "torment" in the Latin phrase *remorsus conscientiae*. In Old French, this became *remors de conscience*, and, by the fifteenth century, it was shortened in English to "remorse."

A related word of various figurative senses is "mordant." As an adjective, it means "biting, sarcastic." As a noun, it refers to a substance that "bites" into a fabric for a permanent dye; an adhesive surface for binding gold leaf to a surface; an acid for etching; crab's claws, and, spelled "mordent," it refers to a musical embellishment in the form of a quick trill that "bites" into the beginning of a note.

All these words derive from Indo-European root *mer-, meaning "to rub away, harm." Less obviously in this family is "nightmare," derived from Old English *niht* (night) and *mare* (goblin causing the feeling of suffocation and bad dreams by sitting on the chest of the sleeper).

Ancient Romans, without the benefit of modern psychological theories, attributed nightmares to demons they called incubus and succubus. An incubus, from Latin *incubare* (to lie on, and source of our word "incubate"), had his way with women in their sleep. A succubus, from Latin *succubare* (to sleep under) positioned herself under the male sleeper. In medieval Europe, union with these demons explained the birth of witches, demons, and deformed humans. According to legend, Merlin, the magician, was fathered by an incubus. In modern psychology, an incubus is the type of nightmare accompanied by a feeling of a heavy weight on the chest and stomach.

sabotage | boot

A seventeenth-century French peasant referred to his wooden clog as a *sabot*. The French verb *saboter* meant to clatter along in noisy shoes, walk noisily, or bungle. *Saboter* formed the basis of the noun "sabotage," which originally described the act of causing a nuisance to create a desired result. The first instances of sabotage may have been revolts against oppressive landowners in which peasants trampled crops with their *sabots*.

In 1887, the French General Confederation of Labor adopted *sabotage* as an instrument of industrial warfare, including the infliction of any kind of malicious damage to injure an employer. These activities included spoiling raw materials, destroying tools, and disabling machinery, to force an employer to yield to labor's demands. It is unlikely, as some believe, that workers threw their *sabots* into machinery; nineteenth-century city dwellers didn't wear these clogs, and sand applied to machine bearings was much more effective than throwing wooden shoes into the gears of machines.

In 1912, striking French railway workers engaged in various acts of sabotage, including uncoupling the *sabots*, which attached railroad car sleepers to other railroad cars, causing great disruption and reienforcing the use of the word *sabotage* in French. "Sabotage" joined the English lexicon in the early twentieth century, as did the noun "saboteur."

Sabot is an alteration of Old French *bot, bote,* source of our word "boot" and modern French *botte* of the same meaning. This word joined our language in the fourteenth century to refer to a large shoe. In the nineteenth century, "boot" acquired the meaning "to kick" (as in "boot the ball") or "eject" (as in "boot out the cat").

As of the twentieth century, when we start up a computer by loading its operating system into working memory, we "boot up," an implicit reference to initiating this process "by one's bootstraps." "Boot up" derives from "bootstrap loader," a short program just smart enough to read a slightly more complex program, which in turn is just smart enough to read the operating system. Thus, in successive steps, the computer pulls itself up by its own bootstraps to operating mode.

Computer users have refined this term to include variants "cold boot" (booting from power-off condition), "warm boot" (booting with the CPU and all devices powered up), "soft boot" (loading only part of the operating system), and "hard boot" (connoting hostility toward or frustration with the computer).

Modern uses of "boot" are literal and figurative: the field goal kicker "boots" the football; the American football quarterback "bootlegs" the ball in a deceptive play, just as "bootleggers" concealed booze in their boots during Prohibition; the baseball player who commits an error "boots" the ball; the fired employee gets the "boot"; and a marine recruit is a "boot" who goes to "boot camp."

The expression "to boot," meaning "in addition, besides," is etymologically unrelated. It derives from Old English *bot*, literally "making better," referring to expiation for a crime or sin, compensation, or remedy. It is related to our word "better." Both "to boot" in this sense and "better" are based on Indo-European root *bhad-, meaning "better."

salacious | salmon

The quality common to the salacious person and the salmon is the ability and penchant for leaping. Although of uncertain origin, "salmon" likely derives from Indo-European root *sel-, meaning "to leap or jump." Latin *salire* and *saltare* both meant "to leap or jump." In Latin, the leaping fish we know as the salmon was *salmo*, genitive *salmonis*. Something that appeals to or stimulates sexual desire (like a salacious novel), and a person who jumps from bed to bed, is salacious. "Salacious" joined the lexicon in the seventeenth century, from Latin *salire*, and originally meant "fond of leaping," as in animals' sexual advances. Salmon are doubly salacious, since they leap upstream for the purpose of mating.

Related words are assail (leap at), exult (when the heart leaps out), insult (jump onto), result (leaps back), sally (sudden attack), sortie (the combat aircraft's flight on a mission), and salient (a feature that projects or jumps out).

Less obvious words derived from *sel- are sauté (a cooking method whereby the chef makes food jump in the pan), somersault

(via Old Provencal *sobresaut*, from Latin *supra* and *saltus*—"jump over") and desultory. A desultory person is disconnected, fitful, jumping from one thing to another. In ancient Rome, *desultores* were circus acrobats who jumped back and forth from one horse to another.

Saltimbocca is a delectable meal of scallops of veal, rolled and stuffed with sage, spiced ham, and cheese, sautéed and served with a wine sauce, so named because the food "jumps into the mouth," from Italian *salta in bocca*. Likewise, saltarello is an Italian dance with a skipping step at the beginning of each measure. Saltation in genetics refers to the single mutation that drastically alters a phenotype.

Salmonella, the bacterium that causes food poisoning, is unrelated to salmon, although you can get salmonella from bad fish. Instead, it is eponymous, from the name of Daniel Elmer Salmon, an American veterinarian who isolated one type of such bacteria in 1885.

salary | sausage

Indo-European *sal- meant "salt." The varied applications of salt to our food yield numerous culinary delights. The Romans liked dishes of assorted raw vegetables in a briny dressing. They called it *herba salata*—salted vegetables—and we call it "salad."

"Sausage" derives from the same *sal- root, by way of Latin *salsus,* meaning "salted," Vulgar Latin **salsicia* and Anglo-Norman *sausiche.* The underlying notion is that the meat in sausage is seasoned with salt. Other salted *sal- foods include sauce, salsa, and salami. A "soused" person is pickled in alcohol.

A less obvious "salt" word is "salary." In the Roman army, soldiers received a sum of money to buy salt, a precious commodity because it preserved food while enhancing its flavor. The word for this allowance, *salarium,* came to designate the stipend or pension paid to soldiers, then to payments made to officials of the empire. If you are "worth your salt," you will earn your salary.

sanguine | sanguinary

To the ancients, and through the Middle Ages, the conception of the link between physiology and emotions was much simpler than today. The prevailing belief was that emotions were governed by four humors: blood, phlegm, yellow bile, and black bile. An excess or lack of any of these humors caused a range of emotional states almost as broad as found in *Diagnostic and Statistical Manual of Mental Disorders,* the psychiatrist's bible for classification of mental disorders.

The word "humor" in this sense is pure Latin for *liquid.* Just as the ancients once believed that there were only four elements (earth, air, fire, and water, eventually adding a fifth, quintessence, for the substance of the stars and planets—see quintessence/fist for more on this), they believed that four liquids in our bodies, known as humors, control our "temperament" (from Latin *temperamentum,* meaning "mixture").

According to the theory of humors, an excess of blood results in a ruddy complexion, thought to be characteristic of a person who is passionate, courageous, ready to fall in love, and full of hope. Our word "sanguine," from Latin *sanguis, sanguin-* (blood), means "cheerfully confident, optimistic." "Sanguine," meaning "bloodred," entered our lexicon in the fourteenth century. The meaning of ruddy complexion is first recorded in the writings of Wyclif as "sanguyn" and in Chaucer's *Canterbury Tales* as "sangwyn." The extended sense of cheerful, hopeful, and confident did not arise until the seventeenth century.

The same "blood" sense is in the word "sanguinary," meaning "accompanied by bloodshed, eager for bloodshed, or bloodthirsty," based on the same Latin root. It was first used in Bacon's *Essays*, perhaps by influence of French *sanguinaire*, on the model of Latin *sanguinarius* (pertaining to blood), in expressing a sentiment as applicable today as when Bacon wrote it in 1625: "We may not . . . propagate Warrs, or by Sanguinary Persecutions, to force Consciences." Many battles in the Civil War can be described appropriately as "sanguinary."

Too much phlegm, the cold and moist liquid, makes a person (depending on the extent of the imbalance), even-tempered, calm, sluggish, unemotional, even apathetic. Today, a "phlegmatic" person has these same characteristics.

Too much yellow bile causes a disposition that is peevish and, literally, ill-humored. Today, "bilious" has the same meaning, as well as the more technical sense of experiencing gastric distress caused by a disorder of the liver or gallbladder, sometimes causing a sickly appearance. A related word is "choleric," meaning "short-tempered," from Latin *chole*, meaning "bile." The obscure word "liverish," meaning "ill-natured, grouchy," is a vestige of the theory of yellow bile, based on the belief that this disposition was a symptom of excess secretions of bile due to a liver disorder.

Too much black bile causes melancholy, a word derived from Latin *melancholia*, meaning "the state of having too much black bile." Today, someone who is melancholy is sad, depressed, or gloomy. The archaic meaning of "melancholy" is "black bile," or an emotional state characterized by sullenness believed to arise from excess black bile. For a related word based on black bile, see up/supine.

As you can see, an imbalance in humors can cause somewhat eccentric behavior, which in certain circumstances stimulates laughter. Today, we have vestiges of the ancient theory of the four humors not only in our words sanguine, phlegmatic, bilious, choleric, and melancholy, but also in such expressions as "he's in a bad humor." We also enjoy the "humor" of comedy routines, many of which are based on "humorous" characters.

The modern use of words based on outdated theories and concepts likewise appears in words based on ancient theories of matter (see quintessence/fist) and astrology (unless you believe in astrology). For words based on astrology, see August/inaugurate, consider/desire, and stun/Thursday.

satisfy | sad

If you are satisfied, why would you be sad? If you ever had too much of a good thing, you would understand the link, in the notion of being wearily sated. Indo-European root *sā- meant "to satisfy," evolving to such words as satiate, satiety, asset, and satisfaction, from Latin satis (enough, sufficient), and to our word "saturate" from Latin satur (full, sated).

"Satire" joins this family of words from related Latin word satura, meaning "plateful of assorted fruit." The notion of a plate of fruit took on a figurative meaning of a literary miscellany as satira, and then the more limited meaning of a literary work of ridicule as our word "satire." For a similar sense transformation, consider that "anthology" (a collection of writings) derives from Greek anthologia, meaning "flower gathering." An anthology is thus, literally, a bouquet of writings.

"Sad" derives from *sā- via Old English saed, meaning "sated, weary." The sense of "unhappy" did not evolve until the fourteenth century. "Sad" acquired a host of meanings over time, in addition to sated, weary, and unhappy. Referring to people, it meant, at various times, steadfast, firm, strong, valiant, trustworthy, serious, dignified, and grave. Referring to things, it meant, at various times, "solid, dense, compact, massive, firmly fixed," and was an adjective for heavy soil, unrisen bread, a dark color, deep sleep, heavy blows, violent fire, and heavy rain. In a curious etymological development, the seemingly intervening senses of "sad" as "steadfast, serious, and firm" first appear at least seventy-five years *after* the sense of "unhappy."

science | nice

Indo-European root *skei- meant "to cut or split." Via Greek *skhízein*, this root evolved into such words as "schism" (a division into mutually opposed parties), "schist" (a class of crystalling rocks that are easily broken apart), "shizoid" (a personality disorder marked by dissociation and withdrawal), and the related "schizophrenia."

The essence of knowledge is the ability to distinguish—to split—one thing from another. Based on this concept, *skei- evolved into Latin as *scire*, meaning "to know," as in "to be able to split one thing from another." If you act with knowledge or awareness, you are "conscious," and if you have inner knowledge you have a "conscience." The word "science" entered the lexicon in the fourteenth century, meaning "knowledge, branch of learning, skill." The modern restricted sense of a branch of learning based on observation, arranged in an orderly system, was first recorded in 1725.

In Latin, if you did not have knowledge you were *nescius* (a compound word combining *ne-* and *scire*). In Old French, *nescius* became *nice*, a word that entered English as "nyce" sometime before 1300, meaning "foolish or ignorant." In Middle English, *nice* had various meanings, including "timid, fussy, fastidious, dainty, extravagant, and lascivious." By the 1500s, "nice" meant "precise, exact, careful, punctilious." The current meaning of agreeable arose in the eighteenth century. Some of the older senses survive in such usages as "a nice shot"; "a nice handling of the situation"; "a job that requires nice measurements"; "a nice distinction"; and "a nice sense of color."

senator | senile

Achieving old age is a mixed blessing: we deserve respect, but don't retain all our faculties. Indo-European root *sen- means "old." From this root evolved such respectful words as sir, sire, senior, but also surly and senile.

In Middle English, *surly* was an alternate spelling for *sirly*, a term of honor for a knight or person of rank or importance. This majestic word, first recorded in 1566, has degenerated to mean "masterful, imperious, arrogant," and then, over time, to mean "sullenly ill-humored, gruff." Likewise, "senile," by this same process of pejoration, degenerated from meaning simply "pertaining to old age" (first recorded in 1661) to its present meaning of impaired memory and inability to perform certain mental tasks because of old age, as in those suffering from Alzheimer's disease. For other examples of pejoration, see bully/friar and cavalier/chivalrous.

In ancient Rome, the senate was the supreme council of the state—an assembly of wise elders. Ambrose Bierce ironically defined "senate" with a sense of senescence as "a body of elderly gentlemen charged with high duties and misdemeanors." Juxtaposing these notions of "senator" and "senile" in one fell swoop, Senator Fritz Hollings offered this explanation for why his fellow South Carolina Senator Strom Thurmond would not retire at age ninety-eight: "The poor fellow doesn't have any place to go, if you think on it. Someone has said the best nursing home is the U.S. Senate."

sherbet | syrup

Unlike other dubious doublets in which the link is not readily apparent, it should come as no surprise that "sherbet" and "syrup" are related. This doublet merits inclusion, however, because of its fascinating etymology.

In Arabic, *shariba* means "he drank" and *sharāb* is a drink, beverage, or syrup. This word for "syrup" evolved to Old French as *sirop*, possibly through Italian *siroppo*, then by the beginning of the fifteenth century to English as "suripe," "sirupe," and "syrop."

Meanwhile, the word that ultimately became "sherbet" was making a similar journey. The same Arabic root is its source, by way of Persian *sharbat*, and Ottoman Turkish *sherbet*. But sherbet has not always been the frozen dessert made primarily of fruit juice, sugar, and water.

The Turkish and Persian words referred to a beverage of sweetened, diluted fruit juice popular in the Middle East and imitated in Europe. In Europe, this sweet juice was diluted with snow. The first record of "sherbet" for this frozen desert is in 1891, although "sherbet" in the earlier sense of a sweet fruit juice was first recorded in 1603. Another word based on this same root is "sorbet," the frozen dessert similar to sherbet.

sherry | jersey

The Caesars spawned more words than any other eponymous source, except the generic "Jack" (see jacket/jack-o'-lantern). The most obvious are the Russian czar, the German kaiser, and the kaiser roll, so named because of its crownlike appearance. Some of our months are named after the Caesars, as discussed in August/inaugurate. Places around the world the Caesars subjugated are named eponymously, such as Caesarea in Israel and Jerez de la Frontera in Spain.

At the time of the Roman occupation, this Spanish town was called "Urbs Caesaris," "the city of Caesar." A Spanish variant of Caesar's name was "Xeres," which, over time, was modified to "Jerez." Sixteenth-century Spaniards pronounced "Jerez" something like "sherris." This town, in southern Spain near Cadiz, is in a region long known for vineyards producing a light wine the British called "sherris," after the town. Over time, the British mistakenly came to believe "sherris" to be plural, and changed the name of this wine to sherry.

Jersey, an island in the English Channel, was called "Caesarea" when the Romans ruled it. "Jersey" is a corruption of "Caesarea," the "-ey" meaning "an island." Thus, "Jersey" is "Caesar's island." Sheep on this island produce wool, woven into "jersey" cloth, made into knitted sweaters we call "jerseys."

The English founder of the colony just south of New York was a native of Jersey, and so he named his new home "New Jersey," the official name of which, to this day, is "Nova Caesaria."

smile | mirror

Ours is not the first generation to smile at ourselves in the mirror. Indo-European root *smei- means "to smile, laugh," whence our words "smile" and "smirk." From suffixed form *smei-ro-, we derive words referring to things that bring smiles to our faces: mirror, marvel, miracle, and mirage. This root evolved into Latin as *mirus,* meaning "wonderful," and our word "admire." When we figuratively "smile together" we are in "comity," that is, in an atmosphere of social harmony.

In his lengthy poem, *Metamorphoses,* Ovid took the concept of self-admiration in a mirror to the extreme. In the story of Echo and Narcissus, Ovid wove a tale of self-love and unrequited love. Zeus had an unsatiable desire to cavort with nymphs. His wife, Hera, understandably disapproved and, in jealousy, followed him everywhere. To distract Hera, Zeus arranged for Echo, a nymph, to engage Hera in conversation. The ruse worked at first, but Hera got wise to this scheme. Because Echo talked incessantly, Hera condemned her forever to wander the earth, unable to speak unless first spoken to, and then capable only of repeating what she heard.

Echo led a sad and lonely existence. One day she encountered young Narcissus admiring his reflection in a clear pool. Echo fell in love with Narcissus but, cursed by Hera, could not express her feelings. In a stunning display of verbal mastery, Ovid tells of this first encounter between Echo and Narcissus, when she saw him "roaming through the country: by chance Narcissus lost track of his companions, started calling 'Is anybody here?' 'Here!' said Echo. He looked around in wonderment, called louder 'Come to me!' 'Come to me!' came back the answer."

Echo knew that actions speak louder than words, but her love was unrequited. Narcissus rejected Echo's advances, as he had rejected the love conveyed to him by all others. Distraught, Echo pined away until nothing remained of her except her voice, which you can still hear today as an echo. In Ovid's words: "Her body dries and shrivels till voice only and bones remain, and then she is voice only for the bones are turned to stone. She hides in woods and no one sees her now along the mountains, but all may hear her, for her voice is living."

Nemesis (source of our word "nemesis," meaning "a source of harm or ruin, retributive justice, or an opponent that cannot be beaten") arranged a cruel fate for Narcissus, which ties in nicely with the relatedness of "smile," "mirror," and "admire": "He saw an image in the pool, and fell in love with that unbodied hope and found a substance in what was only shadow. He looks in wonder, charmed by himself." Just as Echo withered away from unrequited love, Narcissus withered away from self-love. In a fitting ending to his story, Ovid has Echo repeating Narcissus's final words to himself: "She was sorry for him now, though angry still, remembering; you could hear her answer 'Alas!' in pity, when Narcissus cried out 'Alas!' You could hear her own hands beating her breast when he beat his. 'Farewell, dear boy, beloved in vain!' were his last words, and Echo called the same words to him."

As a final act of love for Narcissus, Echo arranged to bury him, making a discovery: "Echo prepared a funeral pile with the dryads, but when they sought his body they found nothing, only a flower with a yellow center surrounded by white petals."

From this heart-wrenching tale we derive the name for the flower with a yellow center surrounded by white petals known as "narcissus." Appropriately named, this flower has narcotic properties. Narcissus's name and our words "narcissus," "narcotic," and "narcolepsy" (a disorder characterized by sudden and uncontrollable brief attacks of deep sleep) all derive from Greek *narke*, meaning "numbness." "Narcissism" is excessive love or admiration of self, a personality disorder characterized by lack of empathy, grandiose fantasies, excessive need for approval, social isolation, and depression. An associated psychiatric phenomenon is acquired situational narcissism, suffered by celebrity athletes and actors. A "narcokleptocracy" is a government in which there is large-scale narcotics traffic, theft, corruption, and violence, and "narcodollars" are acquired from illegal drug traffic. "Narcoterrorism" is violent crime or terrorism carried out as a by-product of narcotic manufacturing and trafficking, especially against enforcers of antidrug laws. In American English, a "narc" is a law enforcement officer who deals with narcotics violations, but in British English a "nark" is a police informer. The British "nark" is unrelated to all these other words, likely based on Romany *nak*, meaning "nose."

Echo's name is appropriately onomatopoetic, and is the source of our word "echo." Even though Echo lost her heart to Narcissus, we can now see into the heart by echocardiography, a diagnostic technique using high-frequency sound waves to produce images of the internal structures of the heart, and we can see inside the brain with echoencephalography. A person who involuntarily and immediately repeats words or phrases just spoken suffers from echolalia. This is a symptom of autism (think of the character Dustin Hoffman played in the movie *Rain Man*), and some types of schizophrenia and the normal occurrence when infants repeat sounds made by others. Bats, porpoises, and some whales navigate by echolocation.

sorcerer | series

Indo-European root *ser- meant "to arrange, attach, join, discuss." From this root, we derive our word for a group of things that are attached: a "series." If someone decides to leave the others in a group, he or she "deserts," from Latin *de-* (opposite of) and *serere* (join). *Serere* is also the source of such words as "insert" and "exert."

Another Latin word derived from *ser- is *sors* (stem *sort-*) meaning "lot, fortune," probably from the lining up of lots before a drawing. *Sors* is the root for such words as sort, assort, consort, and sorcerer.

A "sorcerer," etymologically speaking, is a "drawer of lots." The plural of *sors, sortes,* meant "responses made by oracles," forming the basis for Vulgar Latin *sortarius,* meaning "priest of the oracle," a caster of spells, literally, one who influences lot, fate, or fortune. "Sorcerer" joined the lexicon via Old French *sorcier* as *sorser.* As of 1380, it was spelled *sorceresse* in Chaucer's *House of Fame,* before its assigned lot as "sorcerer."

The word "lot" (*hlot* in Old English, dating back to the tenth century) first meant an object, such as a marked piece of wood, used in an ancient method of resolving disputes, dividing plunder or property, or selecting persons for office or duty. Each *hlot* was placed in a receptacle, which was then shaken. The first *hlot* to fall out indicated who was selected, the antecedent to putting numbers in a hat. Betting in the "lottery" is a similar process, except your number is figuratively in a hat with millions of other people, and your chance of being selected approaches zero.

By the beginning of the fourteenth century, *lott* came to mean destiny by fate or divine provenance, one's portion in life. The sense of drawing lots affecting fate survives in the use of "lot" to mean "fortune" in such statements as "it was his lot to remain a bachelor until he died."

The word "lot" for a plot of land is not recorded until the seventeenth century, in the sense of the plot "allotted" by the king or governmental authority. (In England today, an "allotment" is a small plot rented out for growing flowers and vegetables.) This use of "lot" for a plot of land was followed in the eighteenth century by the generalized sense of a number of persons or things (as in "I'll take the whole lot"), and in the nineteenth century "lot" came to mean a great many (as in "a lot of money").

When you string words together, you create speech. From *ser- evolved Latin *sermo*, referring to a stringing together of words, specifically speech or discourse. By 1200, this word, spelled *sarmun*, had entered English, but with the more limited meaning of a public talk on religion, evolving to our word "sermon." Some etymologists, though, believe that "sermon" derives from Indo-European root *swer-, meaning "to speak or talk," source of such words as "swear" and "answer."

stun | Thursday

In ancient Norse mythology, huge Thor, eldest son of Woden and Frigg, had red hair and a red beard, blazing eyes, enormous vitality, immense strength, and a vast appetite. He had magic gloves, enabling him to shatter rocks. He also had the power to create and command thunderstorms. Thor traveled through the sky in a chariot drawn by two goats, bringing storm clouds. The rattling of his chariot's wheels was heard across the sky as thunder, and the mere shaking of his beard raised a storm. Using his mighty hammer, a throwing weapon on a cord (symbolizing lighting bolts), Thor protected gods and men against giants and monsters. Thor was the Teutonic god of thunder, rain, and agriculture.

Thor's very name means "thunder," derived from Indo-European *(s)tenh- (to thunder). This Indo-European root developed into Latin as *tonare* and, via Germanic *Donner,* to our word for one of Santa's reindeer and the word "thunder." From the Latin we derive "stunned" (thunderstruck), as well as "astonished" (also thunderstruck), and "detonate" (to explode like thunder).

Of the many myths about Thor, one of the most vivid is his encounter with Thrym, a giant who stole Thor's hammer and hid it deep below the earth. Thrym refused to give it back unless the gods sent him Freyja for his bride. In Freyja's place, Thor went to the land of the giants, covered in a bridal veil. This early example of cross-dressing was most effective.

Despite his fierce appearance and red beard, the giants were fooled. They held a splendid bridal feast, with great rejoicing. The giants were surprised by the bride's enormous appetite when she devoured several oxen and more at one sitting. (Think of Paul Bunyan as a blushing bride.) Their plausable explanation: Freyja had fasted and slept for nine days and nights in preparation for her marriage. She would certainly need plenty of energy for her wedding night. This also explained her terrible blazing eyes, which the giants glimpsed through the veil.

The giants prepared for the wedding ceremony. According to legend, Thor's hammer was brought in and put on the lap of Thrym's purported bride as part of the marriage ceremony. Once Thor got his hands on his hammer, he slew Thrym and all the other giants in attendance, returning in triumph.

The delight with which Scandinavians must have recounted this marvelous tale is almost palpable. Indeed, the Scandinavians lived under harsh conditions of early winters and late springs, and so such amusing tales could lighten their burden. Their difficult existence is reflected in words we inherited from them, such as ill, hit, scare, rotten, loose, ugly, wrong, weak, slaughter, and die. But life was not all bad for the Scandinavians. They also gave us the words birth, fellow, trust, and happy.

Our word "Thursday" is in Thor's honor. When "Thursday" first joined the lexicon, it appeared variously as Thorsday, Thoursday, Thurysdage, Thurssdaye, and, making explicit his role as god of thunder, Thundurday, and Thunderday. Other languages derived from Nordic culture likewise honor Thor each Thursday: *torsdag* (Danish), *torstai* (Finnish), *torsdag* (Norwegian), *torsdag-en* (Swedish), *de Donderdag* (Dutch), and *der Donnerstag* (German).

Just as we unwittingly cite Thor's name every time we refer to "Thursday," we cite his parents' names when we refer to Wednesday (Woden) and Friday (Frigg), and his brother's name when we refer to Tuesday (Tiw). (Some etymologists believe Friday is named after Freyja, the Norse goddess of love and beauty.)

The naming logic is astrological. According to the geocentric concept of the universe propounded by second-century B.C. Greek astronomer Ptolemy, which dominated the popular view of the universe through the Middle Ages, seven planets revolved around Earth. Ptolemy wrote a book on astrology, *Tetrabiblos,* which was the authoritative text on the subject for the next thousand years.

According to Ptolemaic astrology, celestial bodies—especially these seven "planets"—influenced human events in the following order: Saturn, Jupiter, Mars, the sun, Venus, Mercury, and the moon. This order was based on how quickly each planet moved from one constellation in the zodiac to the next, from slowest to fastest. The ancients believed that the most distant planet, Saturn, which appeared to move most slowly, had the greatest effect on Earth and its inhabitants. Saturn's slow pace is reflected in "saturnine," meaning "sluggish, gloomy, taciturn," the opposite of Mercury's fast pace, as reflected in "mercurial," meaning "lively, sprightly, volatile."

Ptolemy advanced the theory that each hour of the day was ruled by one of the seven "planets," in the order of their influence. Each day was named for the planet presiding over each day's first hour. The first hour of the first day was controlled by the most distant planet, Saturn, and so the Romans called it *Saturni dies,* literally, "Saturn's day," our "Saturday." By this astrological reasoning, the first hour of each day after Saturn was governed by the sun (Sunday), the moon (Monday), Mars, Mercury, Jupiter, and Venus.

This link to ancient astrology is evident in various Romance languages. For example, Mars's day is *mardi, martedi,* and *martes* in French, Italian, and Spanish, respectively. Likewise, in the same languages, Mercury's day is *mercredi, mercoledi,* and *miercoles*; Jupiter's day *jeudi, giovedi,* and *jueves*; and Venus's day *vendredi, venerdi,* and *viernes.*

When the Germanic people took over the Roman system for naming days of the week after gods, they replaced *dies Martis,* day of Mars, with a day named for Tiw, both Mars and Tiw being gods of war. Likewise, they replaced *dies Mercurii* with a day named for Woden, both gods featuring eloquence, swiftness, and wide range of travel.

It is in this same pattern that the Anglo-Saxons rendered Latin *dies Jovis,* the day of Jove (Jupiter), god of the sky, as the day of Thor. Thus, according to our names for days of the week, Ptolemy was right about planetary influence—a triumph of myth and astrology over science.

tractor | contract

Indo-European root *tragh- meant "to pull, draw, or drag." Via Latin descendant *trahere,* this root evolved into a variety of words, such as the "train" that the locomotive pulls; the "trail" that "traces" the dragged path; the "tract" of land marked out by lines drawn in the earth; the "tract" that is a pamphlet on a political or religious subject; and the "tractor" that pulls by exerting "traction" on a plow or trailer.

When first used in English in 1798, "tractor" referred to a quack device consisting of two metal rods for relieving the pain of rheumatism. "Tractor" did not acquire its present meaning until the 1900s.

The frequentive form of *trahere* is *tractare,* originally meaning "to drag about," then "manage, handle, deal with." From this root evolved "tractable" (easily managed, docile) and "intractable" (stubborn). A less obvious derivative is "treat." From the same Latin root *tractare,* via Old French *traitier,* "treat" joined the lexicon as *tretien* early in the fourteenth century, meaning "negotiate, bargain, deal with," and later that century took on the sense of "handle or deal with in speech or writing, discuss," at the same time "treatise" came into use. The sense of treating with food or drink arose in the seventeenth century, and the extended sense of treating with anything giving pleasure arose in the eighteenth century, as did the medical sense of "treat." "Treaty," from the same root, originally meaning in the fourteenth century "treatment or discussion" and spelled *tretee,* acquired the sense of an agreement between nations in the fifteenth century.

Compounds from this root are "contract" (draw together and, as a noun, an agreement); "attract" (draw to); "detract" (draw away from); "distract" (draw [attention] away from); "extract" (draw out and, as a noun, an excerpt or concentrate); "retract" (draw back); and "subtract" (draw down).

tradition | date

Some forms of giving are acceptable, and others are not. From Indo-European root *dō-, meaning "to give," related but quite different Latin words evolved, both based on Latin *do, dare,* meaning "to give." *Tradere,* combining *dare* with *tra* (across, on the other side, beyond), meant "to hand over, deliver, entrust," and is the source of "tradition." By our traditions, we hand over elements of our culture to each successive generation.

The past participle of *tradere* is *traditus,* from which evolved Latin *traditor,* meaning "one who betrays." The traitor hands over state secrets, and in so doing "betrays" his country and commits "treason," words from the same root.

Many forms of giving are reflected in other words derived from *dō-: donor, donation, condone, pardon, endow, and endowment. A dowager is so named because she is a widow who holds title or property given to her by her deceased husband.

From Greek *didónai* (to give) and *dósis* (gift), we derive dose (something given out), antidote (something given as a remedy) and anecdote. An anecdote, literally, is "something not given out," from *an* (not) and *ekdot* (published). *Anékdota* was the title of memoirs by the Greek historian Procopius, which consisted chiefly of gossip about the court of Justinian. Even though "anecdote" refers to a short account of an interesting or humorous incident, its secondary meaning refers to secret or undivulged particulars of history or biography. As late as the publication of Samuel Johnson's dictionary in 1755, he defined "anecdote" as "something yet unpublished; secret history."

The sense of "publish" as a "giving out" also survives in other words based on *dō-." An "editor," etymologically speaking, "gives out" an "edition" or publication. The Russian word *samizdat* refers to the secret publication and distribution of government-banned literature. It derives from two Russian words, *sam* (self) and *izdatel'stro* (publishing house). Another Russian word derived from *dō-* is *dacha,* the Russian word for "gift," "land," and "country house."

The giving does not stop here. When a landlord agees to "rent" property, the tenant "rents" it, "renders" payment until the end of the lease term, when the tenant must "surrender" the property back to the landlord on the agreed "date." (These "ren" words are all based on Latin *rendere*, meaning "to return, yield," a compound word from Latin *re-*, meaning "back," and *do, dare.*)

"Date" derives from Latin *data* (Romae), the calendar day given out, or decreed, by the ruler in Rome for an event to occur, and the way ancient Romans dated letters. Typical is Cicero's formulaic ending to a letter: *d. pr. K. lun. Athenis*, abbreviation for "*data* [Romae] *pridie Kalendas lunias Athenis*," conveying the idea that his letter was given to a messenger the day before the calends of June from Athens. (The "calends" was the day of the new moon, the first day of each month in the ancient Roman calendar.) Since such a formula was generally employed so often, usually at the close of a letter, the first word of the formula, *data*, became the term for the date.

Less obvious members of this word family are add, die, vend, and data. "Add" derives from Latin *addere*, a compound of *ad* (join together) and *dare*. "Die," the word for the device used to cut out, form, or stamp material, thereby giving it shape (e.g., to make coins), and the gambling cube, derives from **dō-* via Latin *datum*, neuter past participle of *dare*, and Middle English *de*. "Vend" derives from Latin *venumdare*, a compound of *venum* (sale) and *dare*. "Data," plural of "datum," is, literally, the thing given or assumed, and in the seventeenth century acquired the meaning "facts, information."

trivia | triangle

Numerous words based on the concept of three-ness derive from Latin *tres, tria*, including triangle, triplets, trio, tripod, triceps, tricuspid, trident, trifocals, triple, trillion, trinity, trivet, and triceratops (the three-horned dinosaur). If you fear the number thirteen (as in Friday the thirteenth), you suffer from triskaidekaphobia, from Greek *tris* (three) *kai* (and) *deka* (ten) *phobiā* (fear). What is "trivia" doing in this group?

In Latin, *trivium* meant "place where three roads meet," and, more generally, "crossroads." (The Roman goddess of crossroads was named Trivia.) The adjective *trivialis*, which literally meant "pertaining to crossroads," came to mean "common, ordinary," with reference to the subject of ordinary conversation at such a place. The word "trivial" meaning "commonplace" was first recorded in English in 1589. Meaning "not important, insignificant," it first appeared in Shakespeare's *Henry VI* (1593). "Trivia" did not join our lexicon until the twentieth century.

Less obviously related *tria*-based words are tribe, from Latin *tribus,* one of three ethnic divisions of the original Roman State, and possibly tribute. In ancient Rome, a *tributus* was an allotment among tribes. Around 1350, "tribute" entered English as "tribit," a tax paid to a ruler or master for security and protection. Today we pay tribute with words rather than money.

All these words ultimately derive from Indo-European *trei-, or *tris-, meaning "three." A third party, present at an agreement, could "testify" as to its terms, whence testimony, testament (as in the witnessed "last will and testament"), intestate (dying without a will), and all the words from related Latin *testari* (bear witness): attest (bear witness), protest (witness forth), detest (originally "bear witness against"), contest ("call witnesses" against), and testimonial (a witness's declaration of esteem). The same Indo-European root, via Germanic, gives us three, thirty, thirteen, and third.

Other words in this "three" family are "troika," the Russian carriage pulled by three horses (from Russian *troje,* meaning "group of three"), and "sitar," from Persian *si,* meaning "three." The sitar, the most dominant instrument in Hindustani music, has as few as three main playing strings.

tryst | betrothal

A tryst could lead to a betrothal, or it could wreck a marriage. Which consequence follows depends on truthfulness in a relationship, and therein lies the link. Indo-European root *deru- meant "firm, solid, steadfast," with specialized references to trees and objects made of wood. In ancient Greek, *drus* meant "oak tree." Our words "tree" and "tray" derive from this Indo-European root, as do geek-speak "tree-ware" or "dead tree editions" for newspapers and magazines, emphasizing the solidity of these objects compared to the ephemeral nature of "software," which sends messages through the ether. Someone who is steadfast is "true," speaks the "truth" by his "troth" and can be "trusted." In Middle English, *be* meant "by" and *treuth* meant "a pledge," resulting in the compound word *betrouthen,* and our "betrothal." A betrothal then is, literally, a promise "by pledge." When two nations make a pledge to each other they enter into a "truce." Someone who waits trustingly for his or her lover to appear may long for a "tryst" (from Old French, *triste,* meaning "waiting place").

The "solid" sense of *deru- survives in such words as dour, duress, endure, indurate, obdurate (all from Latin *durus,* meaning "hard"), and a variety of "-dendron" words from Greek *dendron,* meaning "tree," such as rhododendron and philodendron.

The "rhodo-" in "rhododendron" means "rose." The "philo-" in philodendron means "loving," as in philology (love of words), philanthropy (love of mankind), philharmonic (love of music), philosophy (love of wisdom), and philately (love of stamps). What does the philodendron love? This tropical plant loves to twine around trees.

One final member of this *deru- family is the druid, so named from Celtic *dru-wid, meaning "strong seer." A druid is a member of an order of priests in ancient Gaul and Britain who, in Welsh and Irish legend, were prophets and sorcerers.

turban | tulip

Unlike most doublets in our English lexicon, this doublet derives from Persian, also known as Farsi, the Iranian branch of Indo-European. The Persian word *dulband* meant "turban." This word traveled the globe: to Turkey as *tülbent* (gauze, muslin, used for turbans), to Italy as

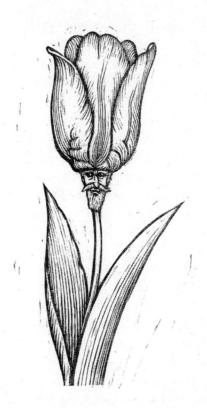

turbante, France as *turbant,* and England as "tolipane," "torbant," and, in the most recent incarnation in its paripatetic adventures, as of the end of the sixteenth century, as "turban."

What does all this have to do with tulips? The same Persian root, *dulband,* and Turkish *tülbent,* traveled to France as *tulipan,* over time shortened to *tulipe.* The sense shift occurred in France, where the resemblance between the headdress and the flower became evident when the flower was imported to Europe in the sixteenth century from the court of Turkish sultan Suleiman the Magnificent. (In addition, Turkish men may have tucked tulips into their turbans.) The Dutch imported the flower and its version of the word as *tulipa.* The first record of the word for this flower in English was in the sixteenth century. It was variously spelled "tulpian," "tulpia," and "tulipa," and was shortened to "tulip" early in the seventeenth century.

Archaic meanings of "tulip" reflect that flower's shape with reference to the flared swell in a gun's muzzle, a bishop's mitre, and an explosive charge to destroy a length of railway track, transforming the parallel rails into a tulip-shaped metallic configuration.

One more point about "tulip": In the 1630s, trading in tulips, free of regulation in the Netherlands, increased to a frenzy of rampant speculation. By 1636, bulbs purchased for a few guilders were sold for hundreds of guilders just a few months later. As the gamble grew wilder, houses were mortgaged to purchase bulbs, and acres of land were exchanged for single bulbs. People in all walks of life were swept up in the craze, selling their businesses and investing their life savings in slips of paper representing future flowers. By 1637, speculation reached such a peak that bulbs were sold faster than they could grow. That year, the market collapsed, leaving many people bankrupt.

The first record in English for the word describing this phenomenon was in 1710, characterizing a person "of good Sense, had not his Head been touched with . . . the . . . Tulippomania." This word survives as "tulipomania" to describe one of the most extraordinary speculative manias in history. In comparison, the 1990s tech-stock boom and bust is a mere dalliance. The irony, of course, is that this mania was not for the tulip itself, but for money, the beauty of the flower lost in the greed-induced frenzy. This mania did, though, give birth to the Dutch bulb trade, for which every tulip lover, whether or not turbaned, is a beneficiary.

uncouth | enormous

Knowledge takes many forms. Indo-European root *gnō- meant "to know." Words directly related to knowledge from this root include can (able to), cunning (artful deception), ken (understanding), cognition, cognizance, connoisseur (person with specialized knowledge), note, connote, annotate, notify, notice, notion, and recognize. "Acquaint" is based on Latin ad (an intensive) and cognoscere (to know). When a doctor uses discernment by differentiating one set of symptoms from another, he or she makes a "diagnosis," from which the doctor can make a "prognosis." Someone who chooses not to know "ignores," and someone who just doesn't know is "ignorant."

An "ignoramus" is an ignorant person. Literally, it means "we do not know," a New Latin word coined in the sixteenth century derived from Latin *ignorare*, meaning "not to know." "Ignoramus" was first used in English as a legal term when a grand jury determined that the evidence presented was insufficient to put the accused on trial. The meaning of "ignorant person" is from the title of a 1615 play by George Ruggle intended to expose the ignorance of lawyers. In the play, the name of one of the lawyers was, appropriately, Ignoramus.

Less obvious *gnō- words include "uncouth," which now means "crude or unrefined," but once meant "unfamiliar or foreign"; and "quaint," which now means "odd in an old-fashioned way," but once meant "clever, cunning, or peculiar." Someone who is widely known, infamously, is notorious.

A "gnomon" is the stylus of the sundial that projects the shadow by which we tell time. "Physiognomy" is a fancy word for facial features, and the art of judging human character from those features.

A series of words derives from *gnō- via the word for the ancient Roman carpenter's square, known as a *norma*, which more generally meant "the commonly known or accepted pattern, precept, or rule." Something within the rule is the "norm" (average), but something outside the norm is abnormal or "enormous." "Enormous" originally had a range of meanings, including "unusual" and "outrageous." It took on the more limited meaning of "huge" in the nineteenth century, although the sense of outrageousness endures in our word "enormity." If knowledgeable parents of a newborn aspire that their daughter develop within the norm, they may call her "Norma." ("Norman" is not in this family though, based instead on "Northman," that is, a Norwegian. This name predates the Norman conquest of England.)

universe | inch

Indo-European root *oi-no-, meaning "one," evolved into an assortment of words, all of which have one-ness as their essence, although not always obviously so.

This root, via Germanic, produced one, once, only, a, an, alone, lonely, any, none, and atone (meaning "put oneself at one with God or with others"). "Eleven" literally means "one left over (after ten)," from Old English *endleofan, end* meaning "one," and *leofan* meaning "left over," source of "leave."

*Oi-no- evolved into Latin as *unus,* source of the word "universe" (everything turned into one). Latin *universitas* meant whole. In the postclassical period, this word was applied to guilds and other such associations, referring to the totality of their membership. These associations included societies of teachers and students, from which we derive the modern meaning of "university." It is also the source of union, unite, unity, unanimous (of one mind), unicorn, uniform, Unitarians, unicycle, unisex, unison (one sound), unique, and unit.

Less obvious cousins in the *unus* family are inch, ounce, university, and onion. A Latin word derived from *unus* is *uncia,* meaning "one-twelfth." From *uncia* we have the measurements of an inch (one-twelfth of a foot) and an ounce (one-twelfth of a troy weight).

The lowly onion has a claim to be a member of this unique family. "Onion" derives from Old English *ynne,* which in turn may stem from Latin *unio,* a word of uncertain origin, but that may be the same as *unio* related to *unus.* In this conception, an onion is a unity formed of many layers.

up | supine

Here is a doublet of opposites. After all, if you are up, you can't at the same time be supine—on your back—even though you are faceup in that position. The explanation lies in the common Indo-European root for this doublet, *upo-, meaning "under, up from under, over." We have a range of words up and down the lexicon based on this root.

On the "up" side are such "up-" words as upheaval, uphill, uphold, uplift, upright, uprising, uproarious, uproot, upside, and upchuck. Less obvious "up" words are above (from Old English *bufan*), oft and often (from Germanic *ufta, meaning "frequently"), and eaves, the projecting overhang at the lower edge of a roof (from Old High German *obasa*, meaning "portico").

In Old English, the place where water fell from the eaves was called the *yfesdrype*. To prevent the rainwater dropping off eaves from injuring a neighbor's property, English law prohibited construction of a house less than two feet from another person's property, an early form of zoning regulation, now known as sideyard and setback restrictions. This space between eaves came to be called the *eavesdrip*, meaning "eavesdrop." By the fifteenth century, people standing in this space trying to hear private conversations were called "eavesdroppers," from which we have the back formation "eavesdrop" for "listen secretly," first recorded in 1606.

On the "down" side are words conveying a down position or subservience, from variant Indo-European form *(s)up-. "Supine" derives from Latin *supinus*, meaning "lying on the back," from the notion of being thrown back or under. "Sub-" words derived from *(s)up- include subconscious, subcontract, subdivide, subjugate, submarine, submerge, submission, subordinate, subpoena (a legal writ requiring an appearance "under penalty" if you don't show up), subrogate, subscribe (literally, to sign at the end of a document), subservient, subsidiary, substandard, substitute, subterfuge, subtract, and suburb.

People in a subservient position derive the name for their status from *upo-, via its extended form *upo-st-o, and Vulgar Latin *vassus* (vassal): valet (one who performs personal services for another), vassal (originally, one who held land from a feudal lord, now a subordinate or dependent), and varlet (originally a knight's page, now a servant or rascal).

Not all "sub-" words point down, however. The "up" sense

from *upo- endures in such "sub-" words as "sublime" and "subli-mation." "Sublime" means "majestic, of high spiritual, moral, or intellectual worth, supreme, inspring awe." Its archaic meaning is "raised aloft, set high." "Sublimate" in chemistry is to transform from a solid to a gaseous state without becoming a liquid. Appro-priately, in light of the up/down quality of *upo-, "sublimate" also means to transform directly from a gaseous to a solid state without becoming a liquid.

All these "sub-" words derive from Latin *sub*, meaning "under." Its counterpart in Greek is *hypo-*, as in hypodermic (under the skin—subcutaneous), hypotenuse (the downward sloping side of a right triangle opposite the right angle), hypothalmus (the part of the brain below the thalmus, which regulates autonomic activities), hypothermia (abnormally low body temperature), hypothesis, and hypothetical (from Greek *hypóthesis* meaning "base of an argu-ment"), hypochondria, and hypocrisy.

"Hypochondria," which means the persistent neurotic belief that one is ill, or about to become ill, derives from Greek *hypochón-dria*, a compound word from *hypo* and *chóndros*, meaning "cartilage of the breastbone." In Late Latin, *hypochondria* meant "abdomen." The abdomen was once thought to be the seat of black bile, the source of melancholy. A person suffering from melancholy may well suffer from hypochondria. For more about the humors, and words that derive from this old theory of medicine, see sanguine/sanguinary.

"Hypocrisy" and "hypocrite" both derive from Greek *hypókrisis*, from *hypokrinésthai*, a compound of *hypo-* and *krinesthai* (to explain), meaning "to play a part, pretend." In ancient Greece, a *hypokrites* was a stage actor, but came to mean a pretender or liar.

Two final members of the downside of the *upo- family derive from Sanskrit. The translucent mineral "opal" derives its name from Sanskrit *upara-* (lower) and *upala-s* (gem), via Greek *opallios*, Latin *opalus*, and French *opale, opalle*, presumbaly because opals are mined from under the ground. The title of the *Upanishad*, the treatises setting forth the theology of ancient Hinduism, is from

Sanskrit words *upa* (under, near), *ni* (down) and *sidati* (he sits), conveying the idea of learning wisdom while sitting at the feet of a master.

verdict | warlock

The common link here is truth and the related concept of oath taking. Before jurors are sworn in, they answer questions to determine their competence and suitability for the case, a process known as "voir dire," from the Anglo-Norman meaning "to speak the truth." The jury's verdict—the announcement of its decision at the end of a trial—is, literally, a true saying. This word was borrowed from *verdit,* the Anglo-Norman variant of Old French *veirdit,* itself a compound of *veir* (meaning "true," from Latin *verum*) and *dit* (meaning "saying, speech," from Latin *dictum*). The first syllable of "verdict" traces its lineage to Indo-European root *wēro- (true), which has such truth-related derivatives as verity, very, aver, verify, and verisimilitude (a fancy word for "realistic quality").

So how does the male version of a witch join such honest company? The same truth telling implicit in "verdict" and "voir dire" is found in the first syllable of "warlock." "Warlock" is first recorded before 900 as Old English *waerloga,* meaning "oathbreaker," from *waer,* meaning "covenant," and *-loga,* meaning "speaking falsely," related to our word "lie." *Waerloga* more generally meant "traitor, scoundrel, damned soul, demon, and monster." By 1400 it was spelled *warlag, waralau,* and *warlo,* and took on the meaning "evil sorcerer"—our "warlock."

The "-lock" in "warlock" is unrelated to the "-lock" in "wedlock," neither of which has anything to do with a fastening device or embrace. The "-lock" in "wedlock" instead derives from an Old English suffix *-lac* expressing activity, the activity here being Old English *wedd,* a pledge. Old English *weddian* is the source of "wedding."

The second syllable of "verdict" derives from Indo-European

root *deik- (to show, pronounce solemnly). Many formal pronouncements trace their lineage to this root, including benediction, dictator, edict, indictment, interdiction, malediction, prediction, valediction, dedication, preach, and policy (as in an insurance policy), as do words involving conduct pertaining to solemn pronouncements, such as juridical, jurisdiction, vendetta, vindicate, avenge, revenge, abdicate, and dictum (the judge's formal pronouncement of the law related to the case).

Less solemn words in this group include token, diction, ditty, addict, condition, contradict, index, indicate, paradigm, and ditto. "Ditto" traces its lineage to *deik- via Latin *dicere* (to say) and Italian *dire* (to say), in the sense of something already said, as in the "said insurance policy." Dittography is the inadvertent repetition of letters, words, or phrases in writing, such as writing "crititics" for "critics." Other examples of dittography are redundundant, and the predicament of the kid who spelled "banana" as "banananana." (Teacher to pupil: "Can you spell 'banana'?" Pupil: "Yes, but I don't know when to stop!")

vicar | wicker

These words have in common the notion of a turn, or change, from Indo-European root *weik-, meaning "to wind, bend." A willow twig bends, and from such twigs we make wicker furniture, so named from Swedish *viker,* meaning "willow twig." A wicket is, literally, a door that turns, from Old Norse *vikja,* meaning "to bend or turn." Someone who bends or is pliant is "weak," and a series of days that turns to the next is a "week," from Old English *wicu, wice,* having the same meaning.

So where is the turning or change for the vicar? A vicar is, etymologically speaking, a substitute or representative, taking the place of the parson or rector. His name derives from Latin *vicarius* (substitute, deputy), via Old French *vicaire.* The same Latin root gives us vicarious (endured or experienced by one person substituting for another, or felt as if one were taking part), vicissitude (mutability), and vetch (a tendril-laden herb, literally "twining plant").

For a similar sense of one person taking the place of another, see the discussion of "lieutenant" in zero/decipher.

war | liverwurst

For a word meaning "war," people speaking Romance languages, avoiding Latin *bellum* (war) probably because of its similarity to *bellus* (beautiful), derived words from Indo-European root *wers-, meaning "to confuse, mix up." From this root we have our words "guerilla" and "war," French *guerre,* and Spanish, Portuguese, and Italian *guerra,* all meaning "war." From this same Indo-European root we derive such words as "worse" (when things get mixed up, they usually get worse), "worst" (as in worst-case scenario) and, in a positive form of mix-up for sausage lovers, "liverwurst," and such grinded meat specialties as bratwurst, knockwurst, and weisswurst, all names derived from German *Wurst,* meaning "sausage." This etymology brings to mind the admonition attributed to nineteenth-century German chancellor Otto von Bismark: "There are two things you do not want to see being made—sausage and legislation."

During the Vietnam War, the North Vietnamese Army used the A Shau Valley as a staging area for their attack on Hue in the 1968 Tet offensive. By the spring of 1969, the American high command decided it was time to clean out the A Shau, a major terminus of the Ho Chi Minh trail.

On May 10, 1969, one of the most fierce and ferocious battles of the Vietnam War began. After ten days of savage warfare, Americans stood atop Dong Ap Bia at A Shau, but at a terrible cost. The various derivatives of *wers- come together in the fact that, after this meat-grinder battle, the scarred and blasted mountain once known as Dong Ap Bia is now referred to as Hamburger Hill.

window | nirvana

If you were one of the Scandinavian invaders in the Middle Ages who settled in England, you would construct a dwelling without benefit of glass for windows, but you would need an opening for light and air. You would also need a word for that opening. Old Norse *vindauga* meant "window." *Vindauga* is a compound of *vindr* (wind) and *auga* (eye): literally, an "eye for wind."

Vindauga and "wind" derive from Indo-European root *wē-, meaning "to blow." From this root we derive such blow-based words as weather (without a blowing wind our weather would remain stagnant), wing (functionless without wind), vent, and ventilate.

Vindauga, a Scandinavian loanword borrowed around 1200, replaced Old English words for "window," *eagthryl* (literally, "eyehole"), first recorded before 899, and *eagduru* (literally, "eye-door"). Our word "window" derives from *vindauga*, even though we insert glass or screens in our windows, blocking or limiting the wind. The poetic sense of a "wind eye" remains intact though, not only in English, but also in Danish *vindue* and Irish *fuinneog*, both meaning "window," and both derived from *vindauga*.

Less obviously related is "nirvana," the Buddhist concept of the transcendent state of freedom achieved by the extinction of desire and of individual consciousness. The notion is that as long as we have delusions of egocentricity, and its resultant desires, we will continue to be caught up in the endless round of rebirths and suffering.

"Nirvana" literally means "blowing-out," from two Sanskrit words, *nir* (out, away), and *vāti* (it blows). The underlying idea is that one must "blow out" his or her egocentricity and individual consciousness before achieving this supreme goal.

witch | vegetable

Indo-European root *weg-, meaning "to be strong, be lively," spawned a diverse group of words all sharing this kernel meaning.

Examples include wake, watch, velocity, vigil, vigilante, vigor, vigorous, reveille, and surveillance. A less obvious example is "bivouac," derived from German dialectal *beiwacht,* originally meaning "supplementary night watch." Today, "bivouac" refers to any temporary encampment, often in an unsheltered area.

"Witch" joins this family of words because of a witch's supposed power to awaken the dead. Her name derives from Germanic *wikkjaz, meaning "one who wakes the dead." The pagan nature religion Wicca derives its name from the same root, via Old English *wicca,* meaning "sorcerer, wizard," even though Wiccans do not endeavor to awaken the dead.

What is "vegetable" doing in this group? Anyone who has ever planted a vegetable garden knows the answer, the link being in the strength of a seed, with the right soil, sun, and rain, to become "lively," growing to fruition. "Vegetable" derives from *weg- via Latin *vegetare* (enliven) and *vegetabilis* (growing, flourishing). Seventeenth-century metaphysical poet Andrew Marvell used "vegetable" in this sense in his poem "To His Coy Mistress" when he tells her that "Had we but world enough, and time . . . / My vegetable love should grow / Vaster than empires, and more slow."

Xmas | X ray

The *X* in Christmas signifies Christ. *X* has been the symbol for Christ in English since at least the twelfth century, when "Christianity" was written "Xianity." The first written record of an early variant of "Xmas" was in 1551: "from X'temmas next following." By the beginning of the nineteenth century, the term was shortened, as in Coleridge's Christmastime letter to a friend in 1799: "My Xstmas Carol is a quaint performance." Two years later, Coleridge wrote: "On Xmas Day I breakfasted with Davy."

The *X* in "Xmas" derives from the Greek letter *X*, pronounced "chi," a gutteral throat-clearing sound. The Greek word that gives us the English word "Christ" begins with *X*, pronounced "Christos." Christopher Columbus signed his first name beginning with an *X*, using Greek and Latin letters meaning "bearer of Christ."

The *X* in R and in Xmas is eponymous. The slant across the *R*'s leg, forming the *x* in the symbol for a prescription, is the symbol for the Roman god Jupiter, patron of medicine. The *R* in " R " stands for Latin *recipe!*, literally meaning "take this!," which is just what the doctor is telling you to do. So when a doctor gives you a prescription, he is ordering you to take medicine, fortified by Jupiter's healing powers. Similarly, a cookbook author is telling you what to do with ingredients in a "recipe," but without invoking those powers.

An alternative theory is that the *X* in R derives from Egyptian god Horus, the son of two of the main gods in Egyptian mythology, Isis and Osiris. Horus's uncle, Seth, murdered Osiris. To avenge his father's death, Horus fought Seth. During this fight, Seth tore out Horus's left eye and ripped it to bits. Thoth, god of wisdom and magic, found the eye, pieced it together, and added magic. Thoth returned the eye to Horus, who gave it to his murdered father, bringing him back to life. The depiction of the eye of Horus became a powerful symbol in Egypt for healing powers, and was worn as an amulet to ward off sickness. This symbol is of an eye and eyebrow, with a marking under it, and may be the origin of R_x, a variant of which you will find on a dollar bill within the pyramid, associated with Freemasonry.

X is the sign for a kiss, for multiplication, for the number ten, for reactance in electronics, for a ten-dollar bill, for an adult film, for dimensions (as in 3' × 4'), for power of magnification (as in 50x telescope), for a signature of an illiterate person, for an axis in Cartesian coordinates, for an unknown, for a kind of radiation that could not be identified initially (Xray), for a former spouse, for captures in chess, for cross-outs, for indicating a choice, and generally for marking the spot.

This letter originated as North Semitic *taw,* meaning "mark," signifying the "t" sound. It was adopted by Classical Greek for the "kh" sound (as in Scottish *loch* and Yiddish *chutzpah*), then passed into Latin and English in its present form and sound.

Ambrose Bierce, in his *Devil's Dictionary,* had his own take on the letter *X*:

> X in our alphabet being a needless letter has an added invincibility to the attacks of the spelling reformers, and like them, will doubtless last as long as the language. X is the sacred symbol of ten dollars, and in such words as Xmas, Xn, etc., stands for Christ, not, as is popularly supposed, because it represents a cross, but because the corresponding letter in the Greek alphabet is the initial of his name.

yoga | conjugal

The underlying concept in this doublet is "joining," expressed in Indo-European root *yeug-. This root evolved, via Sanscrit, to our word "yoga," literally meaning "union" (with the divine), referring to this spiritual discipline to achieve such union. A close doublet is the "yoke" used to join two animals. The Latin word for yoke, *iugum,* later spelled *jugum,* by extension, and with modified spelling *iugulum* and *jugulum,* referred to that part of the body resembling a yoke: the collarbone. To this day, we refer to the vein in the throat along the collar bone as the "jugular" vein. Another derivative of *jugum* was *conjugalis,* source of our word "conjugal," the newlywed's "conjugal bliss," and the inmate's "conjugal visits."

Other words in this family are "join" and "subjugate" (bring under the yoke), conjugate (yoke together the various forms of a verb), adjust (join together by accommodating), junta (people joined together for a common purpose), joint (the place where two bones join together, where people join together to hang out, or where people involuntarily join together in prison), and the less obvious joust (joining together to fight), injunction (a court order compelling someone to do or not do something), and zygote (the cell formed from the union of two gametes, from the Greek *zygón* [yoke]).

The more obscure word "zeugma" (also referred to as "syllepsis") applies to a figure of speech in which a verb is used with two subjects or objects, or an adjective to modify two nouns, although the verb or adjective is appropriate to only one noun. Examples include Dickens's phrase in the *Pickwick Papers:* "Miss Bobo . . . went straight home, in a flood of tears, and a sedan chair," and the sentence: "She caught a cold and a husband."

A final word joining in the *yeug- family is the astronomical term "syzygy." A derivative of Greek *syzugía* (union), from Greek *syn-* (together) and *zygón* (yoke), "syzygy" refers to the point in the orbit of the moon when it lies in a straight line with the sun and earth, or the configuration of the sun, moon, and earth lying in a straight line.

zero | decipher

Both words derive from Sanscrit *śūnya-m,* meaning "empty place, desert, naught," via Arabic translation of this Sanscrit word as *cifr,* meaning "zero." *Cifr* passed into Medieval Latin as *zephirum,* Old Spanish as *zero,* Italian as *zefiro,* and into French as *zèro.* The concept of zero in India was a major advance in mathematics. Some medieval Europeans found zero a frightening and sacrilegious concept, since it implied nothingness and absence. We write Arabic numerals left to right (contrary to the practice in Arabic writing) by influence of the Indian origins of our numbering system. The idiomatic "zero in," meaning "to aim at or concentrate on," is from the "zeroing" of the sights of a rifle, that is, adjusting the sights so bullets hit the exact point aimed at with the shooter making zero estimated corrections in aiming.

The word "cipher" originally meant "zero," then broadened in meaning to refer to any numeral. In the sixteenth century, encrypted communications usually consisted of numbers representing letters, and were thus called "ciphers." "Cipher," and the de-encryption process of "deciphering," joined the lexicon via Medieval Latin *cifra, ciphra,* and Old French *cifre.* (Arabic *cifr* passed into Latin both as *zephirum* and as *cifra, ciphra.*)

Use of the word "zero" for a person of no account dates back to the nineteenth century. "Zip," meaning the same thing, is a derogatory Vietnam War coinage U.S. soldiers applied to the natives they came to "save." It is possibly an acronym for Zero Intelligence Potential, but may derive from an earlier use of "zip" to mean "nothing."

Brazilians have their own zero-based idiom for a person of no account: *zero isquerda,* Portuguese for "zero on the left." A person who is *zero isquerda* is about as useful as the zero in a number standing alone to the left with no decimal point—in other words, truly useless.

The word "zilch" is eponymous, deriving from a never-present but popular character in *Ballyhoo,* an American humor and cheesecake magazine in the 1930s. The magazine featured a series of cartoons depicting scantily clad young women in compromising positions, invariably exclaiming: "Oh! Mr. Zilch!" Since Mr. Zilch was never shown, except as a pant leg protruding from behind a sofa, or as a heap of clothing on the floor, he became the man who wasn't there. By extension, Mr. Zilch became a nothing man and now nothing at all.

Two other words for "zero" are "nought" and "ought." "Nought," also spelled "naught," developed from Old English *nowiht*, a compound of *na* (no) and *wiht* (thing, creature, being). In Middle English, this word was spelled *noht, noght, nought,* and *naught.* *Noghty* in Middle English meant "having nothing, evil, immoral." The milder sense of "somewhat improper" arose in the sixteenth century, and is the source of our word "naughty."

"Ought" for "zero" is an alteration of "nought." This could have been a modified division of "a nought" as "an ought," in the same pattern by which "norange" became "orange," "noumper" became "umpire," "napron" became "apron," "nadder" became "adder," and "nauger" became "auger." Sometimes this process was reversed, as when "an ewt" became "a newt."

The evolution from "nought" to "ought" may have been reinforced by the use of "0" for "zero" as the assumed initial letter of the word of the same meaning. This word was probably also influenced by the word "aught,"—as in the phrase "For aught I know . . ." "Aught" derives from Old English *aht*, a contraction of compound word *awiht*, meaning "anything whatever." To confuse things a bit, "aught" also came to mean "zero," from "an aught," alteration of "a naught." At the turn of the nineteenth century, a common reference to the first nine years of the new century was, for example, nineteen-aught-two, although no one today says twenty-aught-three.

One last word on "zero": love. In tennis, the person who fails to win a point has a score of "love." This expression was used in England as early as the mid-eighteenth century, by which time the British had imported tennis from France. The name of the game probably derives from French *tenez*, the imperative of *tenir*, meaning "hold, receive," supposedly shouted by the server to his opponent to prepare to receive the serve. Related "hold" words are tenacious, tenable, tenure, tenant, the tenor who "holds" the melody, and the lieutenant who literally "takes the place" of another officer. For a similar sense of substitution, see the discussion of vicar in vicar/wicker, and consider the British word "locum." In Britspeak, a locum is a doctor's or clergyman's temporary replacement, short for *locum tenens,* literally "holding one's place."

In French, *l'oeuf* means "egg," which is shaped much like a zero. When the French said *l'oeuf,* the Brits heard "love," and thus "love" became "zero" in tennis. For a discussion of other such Hobson-Jobson words, see chaise lounge/longitude. An analogous expression is "goose egg" for zero, in use since the mid-nineteenth century, and the cricket term "duck" in Australian slang, short for "duck egg," also meaning zero.

An alternative theory: A tennis player who fails to score must be playing for the love of the game, rather than for money, just as an "amateur" engages in an activity just for the love of it. Ambrose Bierce's jaundiced definition of "amateur" is: "A public nuisance who mistakes taste for skill, and confounds his ambition with his ability."

zodiac | whiskey

Indo-European root *gwei- meant "to live," a fundamental concept that produced a host of words based on the notion of aliveness, and the singular characteristic of anything alive—movement.

Adjectives from this root include quick, vivacious, vivid, convivial, viable, and vital. Verbs include vivify, revive, and survive. Nouns include hygiene (from Greek *hygiēs,* meaning "healthy"), quicksilver (the archaic name for the metallic element mercury, for its liquid movement at room temperature), viand (an item of food), viper (literally "bearing live young"), vitamin, biology, amphibian, microbe, zoo, zoology, and zodiac. "Zodiac" derives from Greek *zoidiakòs (kúklos),* (circle) of the zodiac, from *zōidion* (small represented figure), diminutive of *zōion,* meaning "living being."

"Whiskey" belongs in this family of words because it derives ultimately from *gwei- via Old Irish *uisce* (water) and *bethad,* genitive of *bethu* (life), producing Irish Gaelic *uisce beatha* and Scottish

Gaelic *uisge beatha,* Irish and Scots word *usquebaugh,* and our simplified spelling of that word as "whiskey." The same sense of alcohol
as the "water of life" is found in the French word for brandy, *eau-de-
vie,* whereas Russian *vodka* is merely the diminutive of *voda,* meaning "water."

Suggested Reading

Ayto, John. *Dictionary of Word Origins* (New York: Arcade, 1990).

———. *Twentieth Century Words: The Story of New Words in English Over the Last Hundred Years* (New York: Oxford University Press, 1999).

Barnette, Martha. *Ladyfingers & Nun's Tummies: A Lighthearted Look at How Foods Got Their Names* (New York: Times Books, 1997).

Barnhart, Robert K. *The Barnhart Dictionary of Etymology* (New York: The H.W. Wilson Company, 1988).

Baugh, Albert C., and Thomas Cable. *A History of the English Language 5th ed.* (Upper Saddle River, N.J.: Prentice Hall, 2001).

Bierce, Ambrose. *The Unabridged Devil's Dictionary,* edited by David E. Schultz and S. J. Joshi. (Athens, Ga.: The University of Georgia Press, 2000).

Bowler, Peter. *The Superior Person's Book of Words* (Boston: David R. Godine Publisher, 1985).

Bryson, Bill. *Made in America: An Informal History of the English Language in the United States* (New York: Secker & Warburg, 1994).

———. *The Mother Tongue: English and How It Got That Way* (New York: William Morrow, 1990).

Cassidy, Frederic G. *Dictionary of American Regional English* (Cambridge, Mass.: The Belknap Press of Harvard University Press, 1985).

Chapman, Robert L. *American Slang* (New York: Harper & Row, 1987).

Ciardi, John. *A Browser's Dictionary* (New York: Harper & Row, 1980).

———. *Good Words to You* (New York: Harper & Row, 1987).

Claiborne, Robert. *The Roots of English* (New York: Doubleday, 1989).

———. *Our Marvelous Native Tongue* (New York: Times Books, 1983).

Crystal, David (ed.). *The Cambridge Encyclopedia of the English Language* (New York: Cambridge University Press, 1995).

———. *Language and the Internet* (New York: Cambridge University Press, 2001).

Crystal, David, and Hilary Crystal. *Words on Words: Quotations About Language and Languages* (Chicago: The University of Chicago Press, 2000).

Dickson, Paul. *The Dickson Baseball Dictionary* (New York: Avon Books, 1989).

———. *A Collector's Compendium of Rare and Unusual, Bold and Beautiful, Odd and Whimsical Names* (New York: Delacorte Press, 1986).

Espy, Willard R. *Thou Improper, Thou Uncommon Noun: An Etymology of Words That Once Were Names* (New York: Clarkson N. Potter, Inc., 1978).

Farb, Pete. *Word Play: What Happens When People Talk* (New York: Vintage Books, 1993).

Flexner, Stuart Berg. *Listening to America: An Illustrated History of Words and Phrases from Our Lively and Splendid Past* (New York: Simon and Schuster, 1982).

Funk, Charles Earle. *2107 Curious Word Origins, Sayings & Expressions from White Elephants to Song & Dance* (New York: Galahad Books, 1986).

Funk, Wilfred. *Word Origins: An Exploration and History of Words and Language* (New York: Wings Books, 1950).

Garg, Anu. wordsmith.org (a Web site).

Garg, Anu, with Stuti Garg. *A Word a Day: A Romp through Some of the Most Unusual and Intriguing Words in English* (New York: John Wiley & Sons, Inc., 2002).

Geisel, Theodor S. *Oh, the Places You'll Go!* (New York: Random House, Inc., 1990).

———. *On Beyond Zebra* (New York: Random House, Inc., 1955).

Hamilton, Edith. *Mythology: Timeless Tales of Gods and Heroes* (New York: The New American Library, 1942).

Hendrickson, Robert. *The Dictionary of Eponyms: Names That Became Words* (Stein and Day, 1972).

———. *The Henry Holt Encyclopedia of Word and Phrase Origins* (New York: Henry Holt and Company, 1987).

———. *The Facts on File Encyclopedia of Word and Phrase Origins* (New York: Checkmark Books, 2000).

———. *World English from Aloha to Zed* (New York: John Wiley & Sons, Inc., 2001).

Irvine, William. *Madam I'm Adam and Other Palindromes* (New York: Charles Scribner's Sons, 1987).

Kaplan, Robert. *The Nothing That Is: A Natural History of Zero* (New York: Oxford University Press, 2000).

Kacirk, Jeffrey. *Forgotten English* (New York: William Morrow, 1997).

Lederer, Richard. *Anguished English* (New York: Bantam Doubleday Dell Publishing Group, 1989).

————. *Adventures of a Verbivore* (New York: Pocket Books, 1994).

————. *Crazy English: The Ultimate Joy Ride Through Our Language* (New York: Simon & Schuster, 1998).

————. *More Anguished English* (New York: Bantam Doubleday Dell Publishing Group, 1994).

————. *The Bride of Anguished English* (New York: St. Martin's Press, 2000).

————. *The Miracle of Language* (New York: Simon & Schuster, 1999).

Lipton, James. *An Exaltation of Larks or, the Venereal Game* (New York: Grossman Publishers, 1968).

McAdam, E. L., Jr., and George Milne. *Johnson's Dictionary: A Modern Selection* (New York: Pantheon Books, 1963).

McArthur, Tom (ed.). *The Oxford Companion to the English Language* (New York: Oxford University Press, 1992).

McKean, Erin (ed.). *Verbatim* (San Diego: Harcourt, Inc., 2001).

Mencken, H. L. *The American Language: An Inquiry into the Development of English in the United States, 4th ed.* (New York: Alfred A. Knopf, 1963).

Mish, Frederick C. (ed.). *The Merriam-Webster New Book of Word Histories* (Springfield, MA: Merriam-Webster, Inc., 1991).

Moore, Bob, and Maxine Moore. *Dictionary of Latin and Greek Origins: A Comprehensive Guide to the Classical Origins of English Words* (New York: Barnes & Noble Books, 1997).

Morris, William, and Mary Morris. *Dictionary of Word and Phrase Origins* (New York: Harper & Row, 1988).

Ouaknin, Marc-Alain. *Mysteries of the Alphabet: The Origins of Writing* (New York: Abbeville Press Publishers, 1999).

Pei, Mario. *The Story of English* (New York: J. B. Lippincott Company, 1965).

Pickett, Joseph P., executive editor. *The American Heritage Dictionary of the English Language, 4th ed.* (Boston: Houghton Mifflin Company, 2000).

Pinker, Steven. *The Language Instinct: How the Mind Creates Language* (New York: HarperPerennial, 1995).

Pinkerton, Edward C. *Word for Word* (Essex, CT: VERBATIM Books, 1982).

Quirk, Randolph, and C. L. Wrenn. *An Old English Grammar* (New York: Holt, Rinehart & Winston, Inc., 1957).

Rawson, Hugh. *Devious Derivations* (New York: Crown Publishers, 1994).

———. *Rawson's Dictionary of Euphemisms and Other Doubletalk* (New York: Crown Publishers, 1995).

———. *Wicked Words* (New York: Crown Trade Paperbacks, 1989).

Raymond, Eric, ed. *The New Hacker's Dictionary, 3rd ed.* (Cambridge, MA: The MIT Press, 1996).

Rosten, Leo. *The Joys of Yiddish* (New York: McGraw-Hill Publishing Company, 1968).

———. *The Joys of Yinglish* (New York: McGraw-Hill Publishing Company, 1989).

Safire, William. *You Could Look It Up* (New York: Times Books, 1988).

———. *Language Maven Strikes Again* (New York: Doubleday, 1990).

———. *Coming to Terms* (New York: Doubleday, 1991).

———. *Quoth the Maven* (New York: Random House, 1993).

———. *In Love with Norma Loquendi* (New York: Random House, 1994).

———. *Watching My Language: Adventures in the Word Trade* (New York: Random House, 1997).

———. *Spread the Word* (New York: Times Books, 1999).

Schur, Norman W. *British English: A to Zed* (New York: Facts on File Publications, 1987).

Sheidlower, Jesse. *The F Word* (New York: Random House, 1995).

Simpson, J. A., and E. S. C. Weiner. *The Oxford English Dictionary, 2d ed.* (Oxford: Clarendon Press, 1991).

Soukhanov, Anne H. *Word Watch: The Stories Behind the Words of Our Lives* (New York: Henry Holt and Company, 1995).

Traupman, John C. *The New College Latin & English Dictionary* (New York: Bantam Books, 1995).

Tuleja, Tad. *Namesakes: An Entertaining Guide to the Origins of More Than 300 Words Named for People* (New York: McGraw-Hill Book Company, 1987).

Tulloch, Sara. *The Oxford Dictionary of New Words* (New York: Oxford University Press, 1991).

Varchaver, Mary, and Frank Ledlie Moore. *The Browser's Dictionary of Foreign Words and Phrases* (New York: John Wiley & Sons, Inc., 2001).

Watkins, Calvert. *The American Heritage Dictionary of Indo-European Roots, 2d ed.* (Boston: Houghton Mifflin Company, 2000).

West, Paul. *The Secret Lives of Words* (New York: Harcourt, Inc., 2000).

Winchester, Simon. *The Professor and the Madman: A Tale of Murder, Insanity, and the Making of the Oxford English Dictionary* (New York: HarperCollins Publishers, 1998).

Index of
Indo-European Roots